Sergei Tchoban
LINES AND VOLUMES

Encounters with the Architect, Artist, Collector and Museum Founder

 PARK BOOKS

Introduction
7–11

Architecture as Cultural Dimension
13–21

From First Sketch to Finished Building
24–79

Everything Begins with the City
80–145

On Drawing, Collecting and Exhibiting
146–201

The Museum for Architectural Drawing
202–251

Appendix
252–291

Introduction

All drawings shown in this book without an author listed are by Sergei Tchoban.

Information on all buildings can be found in the Appendix.

Introduction

Kristin Feireiss

For more than two decades, I have been following the architectural and artistic oeuvre of Sergei Tchoban. During this time, we have realised a number of exhibitions together, published several books and held countless intensive discussions with each other. Nonetheless it has always been a challenge for me to fully understand the entirety and complexity of Tchoban's work. Yet I was deeply impressed by his manifold talents as architect, artist, collector, curator, exhibition designer, and ultimately the founder of the Tchoban Foundation – Museum for Architectural Drawing.

Let us start with architecture, the heart of his creative work. Attempting to place Tchoban's oeuvre in the architectural and cultural history of the 20th and 21st centuries throws up many questions that cannot be answered in a single sentence. Even noted

Introduction

architectural historians find it difficult to determine the style of his buildings. Whilst one may see references to Adolf Loos in the work of this Saint Petersburg-born architect, another might find a formal kinship to the Russian neoclassical architect Andrey Burov.

Both are right. But how can this be? Although many architectural elements and formal references to old masters can be found in Tchoban's work, associating him with different epochs and styles of architectural history is not enough to explain his consistent, consciously chosen stylistic balancing act, nor can it shine a light on the uniqueness and value of his creative, content-laden concepts. Above all, these differing interpretations fail to touch the core and grasp the fundamental message of Tchoban's architecture.

During an intensive examination of his work I realised that Sergei Tchoban – impossible to pigeonhole in any established category – is not at all interested in the stylistic recognisability of his buildings through the use of a distinctive architectural signature. His varying architectural forms of expression are determined by incorporating the urban context and the physical and historical conditions of each individual location.

Thus, important aspects of his work, such as façade, old and new, material selection, and shifts in scale and ornamentation, should not be considered in isolation. Together they form a model for his vision of the city: an essentially homogenous but consistently contrasting cooperation and coexistence of different typologies, of old and new, of "everyday architecture" and "landmark architecture".

As a result, I had to constantly rethink my approach to Sergei Tchoban's work, and ultimately reconsider the concept of this book. One of the reasons for that was reading the 2017 publication *30:70. Architecture as a Balancing Act* on the history of architecture from the ancient world to the present day, written by Sergei Tchoban together with the writer and architectural historian Vladimir Sedov, where they propose a new theory of the modern city.

The central question posed in this work of architectural history is as follows: what

Introduction

are we looking for and what is lacking in the contemporary architecture of modern cities? For Sergei Tchoban, the answer can be found in a balanced prioritisation of urban locations for iconic architecture (so-called "flagship architecture") and an increase in the quality of everyday architecture in the urban environment – from the modernisation of existing building stock to a diversified, detail-rich configuration of their façades.

Whether an iconic building or highly detailed everyday architecture, Sergei Tchoban's architectural oeuvre proves that he is a master of both disciplines. His buildings never seem isolated in their surroundings. They are always a response to the respective urban context, however unique this may be. Tchoban's approach, in terms of both design and content, always evolves from the analysis, confrontation, or even adaptation – to the point of reinterpretation – of the urban realm. His architecture, highly valued by residents and visitors alike, can only be understood in this way, allowing it to be seen as a significant contribution to urban building culture.

Although this introduction has focused on Sergei Tchoban's architecture and its role in the urban context, the following pages touch on all aspects of his creative work as an artist, collector, curator and museum founder. Over the course of a year, I held four in-depth conversations with him that have resulted in the interviews published here. These interviews are not to be understood in isolation, but in dialogue with the depictions of his buildings and his artistic oeuvre, along with particular exhibits from his collection and images from exhibitions he has realised at museums all over the world.

I hope that this book – at once a reader and a pictorial volume – succeeds in providing an insight into Sergei Tchoban's complex oeuvre and allows the reader to be inspired by the almost inexhaustible creative energy of this exceptional personality.

Architecture as Cultural Dimension

Architecture as Cultural Dimension

Deyan Sudjic

The centre of gravity of the architectural world has moved steadily back and forth in the past decades. A century ago it was probably located somewhere between Vienna and the Bauhaus. Later there was a shift towards Paris, then across the Atlantic to New York and Chicago. Attention after World War II moved to Los Angeles and then to Tokyo. London was at the heart of the educational dialogue when Zaha Hadid had both Rem Koolhaas and Leon Krier as her tutors at the Architectural Association.

Now we need to look to other cities, notably Beijing and Moscow, to get a sense of where the world of architecture is moving. As the result of a wave of construction, these are the places in which new directions are being

Architecture as Cultural Dimension

FEDERATION COMPLEX, MOSCOW, 2017

taken, reputations are made and shaped, and where new ways of working get their first exposure.

The multifaceted Sergei Tchoban, who is an architect, a gifted architectural draughtsman, and what might be called a cultural entrepreneur determined to give architectural drawings the attention that they deserve, is one of the products of that shift. The context of an architecture studio in the old Soviet Union in which Tchoban grew up is perhaps as removed from the realities of day-to-day digital architectural practice as the pen and pencil. But he draws on both to shape his contemporary output.

In many ways this is not so much a philosophical change in direction, as a recognition of realities that are both cultural and economic. The world has multiple centres now, not just one dominant cultural hub. In the first stages of the transformation of both Beijing and Moscow, the key landmarks were designed by architects from elsewhere. But Russia has always had an exceptionally rich architectural culture, both homegrown and – as in the case

Architecture as Cultural Dimension

of Saint Petersburg, where Sergei Tchoban was born, with its baroque and neoclassical masterpieces – imported. And it is that culture which is now once more demonstrating a distinctive contemporary version of architecture.

Tchoban is an architect at the height of an increasingly prolific career. He began to work in Eastern Europe and has subsequently expanded westward. He was educated in Saint Petersburg in the last years of the Soviet Union. He began his career there at a time when the state was still placing strict limits on private enterprise. Subsequently, he moved to Germany and has since built parallel practices there and in Russia with a number of different collaborators. The projects that he has been involved with range from the largest, in the shape of the sleek sculptural glass of the Federation development in Moscow's new business district, which is one of the tallest mixed-use towers in Europe, to the careful restoration of early 20th-century landmarks in Berlin and a modest Russian Orthodox Christian church.

He has assembled an exceptional collection of architectural drawings, many of them from the heroic days of the Soviet Union and its period of experimental architecture, but also from around the world, up to the present day. And he has been generously ready to share them with scholars and galleries and museums. The collection reflects his own personal interests as an unusually accomplished draughtsman. He began his career when ink and paper drawings still defined architecture. Such drawings had multiple meanings and purposes. They were the seductive means by which a building was represented to those who had commissioned it to persuade them to invest. They were the tools that were used by an architect to design a building. And they were the instructions used to convey what and how to build to the builders.

He has built a museum in Berlin to accommodate that collection which, in its form as well as its content, provides a kind of compass with which to interpret architectural drawing, and perhaps also Tchoban's own work. The Museum for Architectural Drawing is both an intriguing work of architecture that

Architecture as Cultural Dimension

RUSSIAN MONASTERY OF ST. GEORGE, GÖTSCHENDORF, 2017

in itself celebrates its content and a unique collection of architectural drawings, and it is also a representation of the act of drawing. Its content provides an alternative architectural history of the 20th century in its connection of revolutionary Moscow with the present day.

A museum that is the creation of a single individual architect has few precedents. John Soane in the 19th century with his collection from Hogarth to Ancient Egypt, accommodated in his own intricately adapted home in Lincoln's Inn Fields, and its heritage of Joseph Gandy's drawings was clearly an inspiration. But there are few other models.

Tchoban's collection, and the building, designed in partnership with Sergey Kuznetsov, made to house it, a "dignified space" as he has described it, celebrates not simply Tchoban's own passion for drawing, but also the continuing relevance of drawing itself. The collection and the way in which it is displayed make a persuasive case. To see the drawings, which were used to conceive a building whether realised physically or not, is to feel a remarkable closeness to the individual who made them.

Architecture as Cultural Dimension

The quality of the lines, the technique used to make them, the annotations, the state of the paper, are all so revealing of the mind behind them, and the circumstances in which an individual worked. They show the intentions behind a project, which are sometimes lost or hidden in a physical realisation of a design.

Tchoban does not claim an overt connection between his own work and that of the architects whose drawings delineate his personal collection. But there are intriguing parallels to be made. Boris Iofan, who was also a great draughtsman in charcoal and ink, is one of the stars of Tchoban's collection. He was responsible for the Soviet pavilions at the Paris World's Fair of 1937, and at New York in 1939. Tchoban, in partnership with Sergey Kuznetsov, who went on to become Moscow's City Architect, has produced, among other highly significant representative projects, the Russian pavilion at the Milan Expo of 2015, which tells us that such symbolically charged commissions, and the drawings that represent them, have lost none of their fascination for architects and governments.

Architecture as Cultural Dimension

RUSSIAN PAVILION, MILAN EXPO 2015, MILAN, 2015

Four conversations between Kristin Feireiss & Sergei Tchoban

Part 1
From First Sketch to Finished Building

Part 2
Everything Begins with the City

Part 3
On Drawing, Collecting and Exhibiting

Part 4
The Museum for Architectural Drawing

From First Sketch to Finished Building

Part 1

KRISTIN FEIREISS AND SERGEI TCHOBAN IN CONVERSATION

You have an international reputation as both an architect and an artist. But unlike the architects Hans Poelzig or Le Corbusier, for example, whose sketches, drawings, paintings and sculptures are creative works without a direct relationship to architecture, your architectural output is inseparable from your artistic work, since your drawings, aquarelles and pastels always relate to architecture and the city. In order to be able to understand your entire oeuvre, I would like to begin by talking about the design process and the role the sketch plays within it. What happens when you sketch your initial ideas?

Initially, the design process evolves from the way I want to approach the respective project or assignment and where I am at that moment. I'm one of those people who always has a sketchbook to hand, in a size that easily fits in my jacket pocket. Sketchbooks are an indispensable item for me, they are my most important companions – along with my black marker pens. When I'm talking to someone, either in person or on the phone, I will often take out my sketchbook and start drawing, in order to visualise what we are talking about in the form of a sketch. It is a habit of mine, or you could say it's my way of working, but it often proves to be very helpful in the design process. Most of the time I will then take a photo of the sketch with my smartphone and email it directly to my staff, partners, associates, planners and sometimes the clients.

"I learned to love architecture through drawing."

From First Sketch to Finished Building

Can you give me a recent example?

Yes, of course. I recently met with the Russian theatre director Alexander Molochnikov from the famous Moscow Art Theatre, and, as ever, I had my sketchbook with me during the meeting. It was about the set design for the first performance of the drama *The Bright Way. 19.17* for the 100th anniversary of the October Revolution. We were sitting opposite each other in a café and he was telling me about his ideas and how he envisioned them in spatial terms. I spontaneously got out my pad and made a sketch, and it seemed to correspond exactly to what he'd imagined. I then photographed what I'd drawn and, at his request, sent it directly to his co-author. Alexander was quite surprised by this unusual, and for him unfamiliar, method of working.

DRAWING, 2018

From First Sketch to Finished Building

SET DESIGN FOR THE PLAY "THE BRIGHT WAY 19.17" AT THE MOSCOW ART THEATRE, PASTEL ON PAPER, 2017, TCHOBAN FOUNDATION

"THE BRIGHT WAY. 19.17", MAT (MOSCOW ART THEATRE), MOSCOW, 2017

It is quite an uncommon way of working, but somehow logical since sketching is a vital means of communication from which you can develop further ideas in the conversation. You could call it a verbal, hand-drawn-digital form of communication.

For me, the thought process, the creative process, originates in the sketch. The idea flows straight from my head to my hand – in actual fact it happens simultaneously. The interplay between a hand-drawn sketch and the direct, digital communication of it has become another important, indispensable element of the design process for me. This half-drawn, half-digitised kind of approach is an interesting new development in the creative process, especially in the increasingly mobile working world of the architect. When I'm not in one of my offices in Berlin or Moscow, then that's my method of communication. It's how my initial ideas get from my sketchbook to the desired recipient: via smartphone. A third of the messages I send on my smartphone, by email or WhatsApp, are photos of my sketches. For me, this practice is now an indispensable part of my professional communication.

I'd like to come back to the set design of The Bright Way. 19.17. *Is it your first stage design assignment?*

Yes, it's the first time I've designed a set and it's a new and wonderful challenge for me. I made a number of large-format drawings and images for this fascinating project. But before they could be realised, the designs had to be reviewed and passed by the theatre's art advisory board. I was extremely happy when they approved them.

SET DESIGN FOR THE PLAY "THE BRIGHT WAY 19.17" AT THE MOSCOW ART THEATRE, PASTEL ON PAPER, 2017, TCHOBAN FOUNDATION

"THE BRIGHT WAY. 19.17"

The fact that we began our conversation talking about your designs for a theatre set is somehow indicative of your creative output. It shows the broad spectrum of your oeuvre: from drawing as a form of creative expression and devising theatre sets to your work as an architect and urban planner. Despite the differences in these activities, do you still see similarities?

Yes, I do. There's a fundamental, deep-rooted relationship between art and architecture. I learned to love architecture through drawing.

My interest in the urban environment and the purposes I assigned to the buildings within urban structures also came about through drawing.

I would even say that I'm not always primarily interested in the individual building but the context which it is in – the houses to the right and street to the left. For that reason, a building's relationship to the city is of central importance to my approach to a design. The question is: what role does the building play within the urban fabric? I like to compare it with the actors' parts in a play. There are a few leading roles; they are of great significance and carry the entire play, and then there are many supporting roles that perform in a subordinate way, but without whom the "stars" wouldn't be able to unfold. And what's vital for me is that all of them, both the leading and the supporting roles, are equally responsible for the overall success of the work – in theatre as in architecture and urban design.

Is that wishful thinking or do you have an example of how this can be achieved?

When designing a building, I believe that all aspects should be placed into a dialogue with each other from the very outset. As strange as it may sound, I first envisage the three-dimensional appearance of my design, as though I were walking through the city looking at my imaginary building. I reflect on how it would be perceived within the urban landscape, how I as a draughtsman would perceive it in the urban landscape, if it fulfils its intended purpose, and much more. These factors determine the scheme of the building: the floor plans, its form, structure and materiality. For me, this complex, holistic approach at the beginning of a project defines the design process.

Let us stay with the design process, something that involves a wide range of phases and procedures. I'm trying to imagine it as a non-architect: you receive a brief to devise a residential building, design a museum or build an office block or a hotel; regardless of whether it's a direct commission or a competition, there are always distinct building typologies with different uses and users, and they always involve complicated processes. How do you approach this?

I can best describe it using a specific example. I was recently commissioned to build a new Jewish community centre in the USA. It wasn't a big building, but it was still a very interesting assignment for me. On the plane to the USA I got out my sketchbook and, using the documents I'd been given for the project, I made a few preliminary sketches of the building. Shortly after I arrived, I went to look at the site and took in the area. I thought about how the building would stand in relation to its urban context: should it be unobtrusive or make itself more noticeable through a welcoming gesture?

HAMBURGER HOF, BERLIN, 2010

PATIO HAMBURGER HOF

LIVING LEVELS, BERLIN, 2015

LIVING LEVELS

MUSIC AND LIFESTYLE HOTEL NHOW, BERLIN, 2010

VIEW FROM THE WATERSIDE PROMENADE OF THE RIVER SPREE

From First Sketch to Finished Building

CHABAD LUBAVITCH JEWISH COMMUNITY CENTRE, BERLIN, 2007

When you build in a city, the plot is mostly pre-specified – it's located in a block with a clearly defined front and rear side. In such cases, you have to concentrate on the details of the inner structure from the very outset. It was different with the Jewish community centre; the fundamental form wasn't predetermined. There was freedom to choose how representative the front facing the street should be – narrower, wider, articulated or flat. There was also freedom to decide how the specified uses would be accommodated within the space.

What were the major challenges regarding the spatial programme?

A major aspect was the arrangement of the public and the private functions. There are diverse, clearly defined public spaces, like the synagogue room, the reception areas and the dining halls, and then there are the private rooms for the rabbi and his family. The question was whether the public and the private spheres should be connected to or separated from each other.

Such a project calls for an extensive knowledge of Jewish traditions, customs and rituals.

That's true, but it's not the first time I've had to turn my attention to such a topic. For the Chabad Lubavitch Jewish synagogue and community centre in Berlin, we intensively prepared for the assignment by inviting religious studies scholars to the office. Since then I have also designed a Jewish school for the same community. And I was recently invited to take part in a closed competition for a Jewish community centre in Munich. I think the Chabad Lubavitch synagogue and community centre – incidentally the most-visited synagogue in Berlin – was the reference project for my being invited to design the one in the USA. But to come back to your question, I already had experience

From First Sketch to Finished Building

PORTAL OF THE CHABAD LUBAVITCH JEWISH COMMUNITY CENTRE

in this field, so this type of assignment wasn't completely new to me. You are absolutely right though, that one needs to research a great deal in advance for such projects. But that's necessary with nearly all projects, if not always to such a degree. It's often the case in our profession that an architect is only commissioned if the client knows they are familiar with such an assignment or is at least convinced that the architect they choose will find the best solution, even if they don't have the relevant experience.

After you have made the initial sketch, for example while you're on the plane, like with the Jewish community centre in the USA, what happens next and when do you approach your team with a project?

The design process, as I just described it, with all the aspects I mentioned, is my responsibility. It is a fluid process, one that also involves the spatial allocation concept and the schematic floor plans. For example, how the rooms need to be arranged in relation to each other to create a representative entrance and foyer area stretching across multiple floors or conversely how to make it more private. This then gives rise to a sequence of rooms. Sometimes I realise that certain design ideas I had in my head at the outset don't actually work because the usage plan doesn't allow for it. And then, in a dialogue between the spatial configuration and the visual appearance – two steps forward, one step back – a series of sketches is created. Then it depends on how ready I feel the whole thing is before I discuss it with my employees. It's quite common to end up with more than one design: sometimes there are three or four alternatives, all of which I consider viable. Then I have a problem. Normally I know straight away when I've found the right solution that has evolved from the spatial sketches, the floor plan and the functional drawings: it's the only one I want to realise.

ENTRANCE HALL OF THE CHABAD LUBAVITCH SYNAGOGUE

INTERIOR WITH THE INCLINED GALLERY

"It is essential for me to seek and find my own answers regarding both content and design."

Is that the moment the team comes into play?

The project team will already have been chosen in advance. I'll know which people from my office I want to work with on it. Initially it will be a maximum of two employees. I will discuss the whole thing with them again, and they smile when I say, "Couldn't it also be like this, or maybe like this …?" Expanding the team is a gradual process. This dialogue with my team is hugely important to me, and of course there are colleagues whose opinion and experience I particularly value, as well as their clear, constructive and open manner in facilitating a productive exchange of ideas. At the respective project team meetings – and several projects are often being worked on at the same time – I try to find out how my idea has been received, if it's been understood or if my line of thought has gone astray in some way. It's very helpful to employ a dual or triple control method. Having said that, there shouldn't be too many team members in this first stage. It's different in the next phase, in which the team draft the sketches more accurately in order to check if, and to what extent, there are any errors in the initial sketches. This is how, step by step – of course with some setbacks along the way – we progress from the problem to the solution.

The way you describe it would mean – which is certainly not the case in all big offices – that you personally sketch the initial design ideas for each of your ever-increasing number of projects. Is it always you that makes the first draft?

Yes, it is, even though I wouldn't necessarily call my office "big" – "bigger" at most. We now have a staff of around 70 in Berlin; in Moscow it's well over a hundred. For me, the increasing number of projects doesn't alter the fundamental principle: the initial impulses and design philosophy are defined by me.

OFFICE TCHOBAN VOSS ARCHITEKTEN, BERLIN, 2017

From First Sketch to Finished Building

CONVERSION OF THE OFFICE TCHOBAN VOSS ARCHITEKTEN, BERLIN, 2002

If I am completely honest, I think this is the most important thing in our profession. As an architect, it is essential for me to seek and find my own answers regarding both content and design. I am of the opinion that there are much bigger assignments still to come, and I have the desire and the need to keep evolving. You can only develop yourself further when you personally take on the assignments that come your way. For that reason, I simply don't see delegating at the first stage of the design as an option. Still, I give my employees every opportunity to prove themselves and to develop, as a positive, trusting atmosphere within the office is of utmost importance to me.

Do you sometimes hesitate when taking on a new assignment?

For me, every new assignment, every new design, no matter how much experience you have, is a bit like a test, and sometimes you want to shy away from it. Then you have a choice: you can either back out of it and say, "okay, that didn't work", or you take on the responsibility and attempt it again and again until your design concept is consistent with what is actually being demanded in terms of space and detail. There are sometimes things you just don't consider in the dreams of your designs.

That's understandable – even if one isn't a dreamer – given the many, often completely different, commissions that come your way.

That's true, but even with a single task it might suddenly become apparent, for example while doing a scale drawing, that some details just don't fit – from the site plan of a larger building to inaccuracies in smaller projects.

Referring to the general design process, we have just reached the point where all members of the project team, with their respective know-how, have become involved, as well as experts from related disciplines. When do you apply new and innovative techniques? When does the topic of sustainability become relevant?

As I mentioned, designing is a complex process with numerous questions that need to be answered: questions of sustainability, questions of how well a building ages, questions of maintenance, questions of material selection or which surface to choose, and questions about the users and their needs – each individual decision has consequences. I try to keep all these factors in mind when I'm developing a design, even though I don't talk about them with my employees or clients until later, because many ideas occur during meetings. These conversations can sometimes be quite a challenge, especially if the client suddenly says: "I also want this and that". In such situations you have to be careful not to let yourself get drawn into doing something you don't actually believe is right. Over the years I've learned not to react too quickly, and that sometimes it's better to wait for a more suitable time regarding certain points. It's often a balancing act, because you can't afford to miss the moment that the conversation might take a wrong turn, which can potentially make the way back more complicated. This demands a high level of concentration.

Can you give me an example?

I can give you the skin of the building as an example. Apart from aesthetic considerations, the choice of material has a direct influence on the building's energy efficiency, on the construction costs, and so on. So it's important that you and your team are always abreast of the latest developments in science and technology. If you think about the maintenance of a building, for

"Designing is a complex process with numerous questions."

From First Sketch to Finished Building

CITY QUARTIER DOMAQUARÉE, BERLIN, 2004

instance, you have to be aware that different materials require different levels of maintenance. And when it comes to the form of the building, you know that not all shapes can be produced for the same cost and that they don't age at the same rate. That doesn't mean that you should only build inexpensive buildings, but it's important to always consider these relationships. Right down to the structure of the façade skin.

Why don't you simply refer to it as the façade?

I use the word façade reluctantly, because the façade is only seen as an external layer. And, according to the layperson's understanding of the term, there aren't any pure façades in architecture nowadays. The façade is not mere decoration, it is a structural component of the building.

I'd like to go back to the subject of the client. In the 1990s, an edition of the Deutscher Werkbund magazine Werk und Zeit *– which I was working for at the time – was dedicated to the client. Peter Behrens' work with the AEG was considered a paragon of the collaboration between architect and client; today perhaps Vitra and Novartis are such examples. In general, though, there is a widely held belief that the client is to blame for everything. Regarding his housing development at Lützowplatz in Berlin, for instance, Oswald M. Ungers never got over the fact that he was unable to assert his plans against the will of the client. Ungers' building has since been demolished and replaced with a new one. What kind of experiences have you had with your clients? Does a dialogue take place? What can clients bring into the design process? There are architects who believe something like: "I have designed something quite brilliant: they'll either use it because I know it's the right solution, or they'll reject it." Is it the same for you?*

From First Sketch to Finished Building

OFFICE BUILDING AT LENINSKY PROSPECT, MOSCOW, 2010

If we're honest, that's how all architects think and I'm no different. I don't think there are any architects who have misgivings about their designs when they go to meet their client. Besides, you can't convey your ideas convincingly if you don't fully believe in them yourself.

And what about openness and a willingness for dialogue with the client?

Being convinced of one's own design doesn't exclude an openness towards the client or contractor. Quite the opposite, in fact. A doubt expressed by the other party is always based on something, even if they are unable to formulate it precisely. And it is my job – and that of any architect – to take such things seriously and not ignore them, but to try and understand why such a particular suggestion hasn't been well received. You have to figure this out and provide an appropriate solution. That's the core essence of our profession. But before you reach this point, you have to present the whole design, and in our office, I consider this to be my task. I attach huge importance to the presentation of each project and always try to follow a definite logic. I start with the site, explain the references to the surroundings, and outline all the aspects that influenced me to approach the design in the way I did – from the overall concept down to the detail. This is something I prepare in advance with my employees. Sometimes I even go as far as making a screenplay for the presentation, which allows me to precisely define the process. But not a screenplay with words, one with drawings.

GRANATNY ALLEY RESIDENCES, MOSCOW, 2010

KRONPRINZENGÄRTEN, BERLIN, 2017

From First Sketch to Finished Building

SEASONS ENSEMBLE, SAINT PETERSBURG, 2013

Can you help me visualise this?

I reach a moment in my presentation when I demonstrate the impression a normal person would get of the building I have designed before they enter it. Sometimes I use various examples to illustrate this. I give the client the opportunity to ask questions, to deliberate, to choose, to check, to think again or to have their initial decision validated. For me, a prerequisite in this process is that I myself am 100 per cent satisfied with all the solutions I present. As I have said, every presentation – and I don't differentiate between small- and large-scale projects here – is equally important and needs to have a very clear structure. It has to show a path that can be followed by anyone you are giving the presentation to, whether that's the client or a member of the public. It's important to me that they can clearly understand its logical structure and that their approval or criticism is within the framework of this logic. This method encourages constructive discussions and prevents misunderstandings. If I'm honest, I try to make sure nothing is left to chance in these presentations.

What role does the model play for you in the design process? It's something you haven't mentioned yet. There are two fundamentally different approaches to designing. Architects from the American West Coast, for example Los Angeles or San Francisco, primarily produce their designs with the aid of working models. Instead of making initial sketches, they produce models – usually quite plain and made from grey cardboard. Frank O. Gehry works in this way, for example, or Thom Mayne, Morphosis, Erik Owen Moss, and many other West Coast architects. In all the exhibitions that I have realised with Frank O. Gehry over the decades, at the Aedes Architecture Forum in Berlin or the Netherlands Architecture Institute in Rotterdam, the beginning of the design process was characterised by a large number of cardboard models – ten, twenty, or more. Architects from the East Coast, on the other hand, from New York, Boston and Philadelphia, like Peter Eisenman, Bob Stern and Richard Meier, all use the sketch as the starting point for their designs. Some architectural theorists argue that the reason for this different approach to the design is due to the different formal languages, and that the so-called deconstructivist, sculptural architecture of the West Coast is allowed to develop more through the medium of the model. I'll come back to my question: what role does the model play in your design process?

The model is an integral component of the design process for many architects, and for me as well. That being said, I personally prefer to work with sketches and drawings. For some buildings, especially when they are isolated in their surroundings and are therefore able to take on a sculptural appearance, the model plays a very important role – in both the design and the presentation. I have experienced cases in which a client has suddenly been won over by the presentation of a model. It's often the case that the public, too, has to be convinced, and in this context a detailed model of the project is really quite helpful. For many architects the so-called sculptural model is an important means of expression, because many unexpected ideas are generated through the process of sculpting. There are architects who are also sculptors – I'm unfortunately not one of them – and there are those that are veduta painters. I'm more of a veduta painter. At the Russian Academy of Arts in Saint Petersburg, where I studied, they offered sculpture as a subject, but I wasn't a big fan of it even then, although I knew how important it was for one's understanding – in the literal sense of "grasping" architecture. When you sculpt a face, you don't just see the outer visage, you intuitively feel the skull beneath. That's actually the same with a building: you simultaneously perceive the façade and sense the structure behind the façade. These were important insights and

From First Sketch to Finished Building

ARCHITECTURAL MODELS, TCHOBAN VOSS ARCHITEKTEN, BERLIN, 2019

experiences that I also learned myself. Personally, I'm convinced that my drawings also achieve a three-dimensionality. But I have to qualify that by saying I've never designed particularly sculptural buildings, ones that can't be imagined using sketches alone. That's just not my style.

We have been talking about the drawing and its significance. The French philosopher Jacques Derrida wrote that "a small sketch can sometimes achieve more than a large house". Do you agree with him?

To stick with Derrida's words: there's no doubt that a small sketch can be hugely expressive and contain many innovative ideas; unfortunately, there are far more inspiring sketches than there are well-made large houses. However, it's much more difficult to create houses that are successful in the same way, and their makers deserve a huge amount of respect.

Many years ago, at the Aedes Architecture Forum, we put on an exhibition with Gustav Peichl, an old master of Austrian architecture, who incidentally is also an extremely talented illustrator and caricaturist. When I went to see one of his buildings with him, he pulled a small sketch out of his pocket and said proudly: "Have a look at this: that's how I designed it, and that's exactly how it turned out!" This is different to Zvi Hecker, for example, the Berlin-based Israeli architect with whom we realised an exhibition on his Heinz-Galinski Jewish school in Berlin. There were changes to the building from the very beginning of the construction process until shortly before it was completed, because for him the design process wasn't concluded with the finalisation of the technical drawings. These are two quite different approaches: which one is most similar to yours? Does it ever happen that changes are made to your projects during the construction process?

Not so much changes as interventions. Recently, for example, I was at the construction site of my exhibition pavilion at the Tretyakov State Gallery in Moscow. Not a big project, but there were a few complicated details. On site I was much more able to imagine how things would be. There were some MDF panels lying around on the ground, and I made a series of sketches on them in order to show the construction workers on site how the individual details fitted together. But in this sense, they weren't really changes. It doesn't really matter to me if the finished building is in principle the same as my initial sketch – that may be the case, but it doesn't have to be. A great deal is possible within the design process. But it's important for me that there are no fundamental changes after the conclusion of this process, as then the project has to be implemented. It might sound somewhat cynical, but when we're stuck in the middle of a project, I sometimes say to my colleagues: "We'll make the next mistake in the next design." It's true that every idea, every design contains errors that can be criticised in some respect; there will always be one aspect that hasn't been considered. But if you have mapped out a particular concept right down to the smallest detail and always have a certain consistency in mind, then the project has to be realised in this way too.

What does a normal day in the office look like for you, if there is such a thing as a normal day?

In order to structure my time efficiently, I tell my employees in Berlin and Moscow not to include me in any appointments for which I'm not needed. Firstly, it's lost time for me, because my staff can conduct these meetings themselves, and secondly, I have to get my clients used to the fact that I can't always be present in my function as a lead architect and head of the company.

PAVILION FOR THE TRETYAKOV GALLERY, MOSCOW, 2017

From First Sketch to Finished Building

VIEW FROM THE INSIDE OF THE PAVILION

If it's about decisions regarding the design, however, I wouldn't leave it to anyone else. I always do this myself. It might happen that despite everything you don't achieve the result you wanted, but then you know that you have done everything that you believed was necessary. If you still didn't achieve it, then okay, you can learn from that. Since meetings regarding the design are much less frequent than regular meetings, I subsequently have more time. I try to add this extra time to the internal design meetings.

What happens in these meetings?

Each team presents the progress of their project at given intervals and structures the questions that are still open. Due to our longstanding and intensive collaboration, everyone knows what's important to me and every project manager has their own list of questions about the area they're responsible for. We then go through these lists systematically. If I can provide a satisfactory answer to 80 per cent of the questions I'm asked in a given day, then that's a good outcome. Frequently, my answer takes the form of a sketch, or there might be three alternatives and I'll choose which is the right option. This all happens at a rapid pace – blow-by-blow, so to speak. Of the more complex design meetings, for which I schedule around 30 minutes, there might be eight to ten on a more difficult day.

That sounds like a marathon.

Sometimes it seems that way to me, too. It is quite a condensed way of working. When I'm travelling from one meeting to the next, I'll often still be thinking about whether I've answered all the questions correctly, and sometimes, if I realise there's a better solution, I'll begin sketching it.

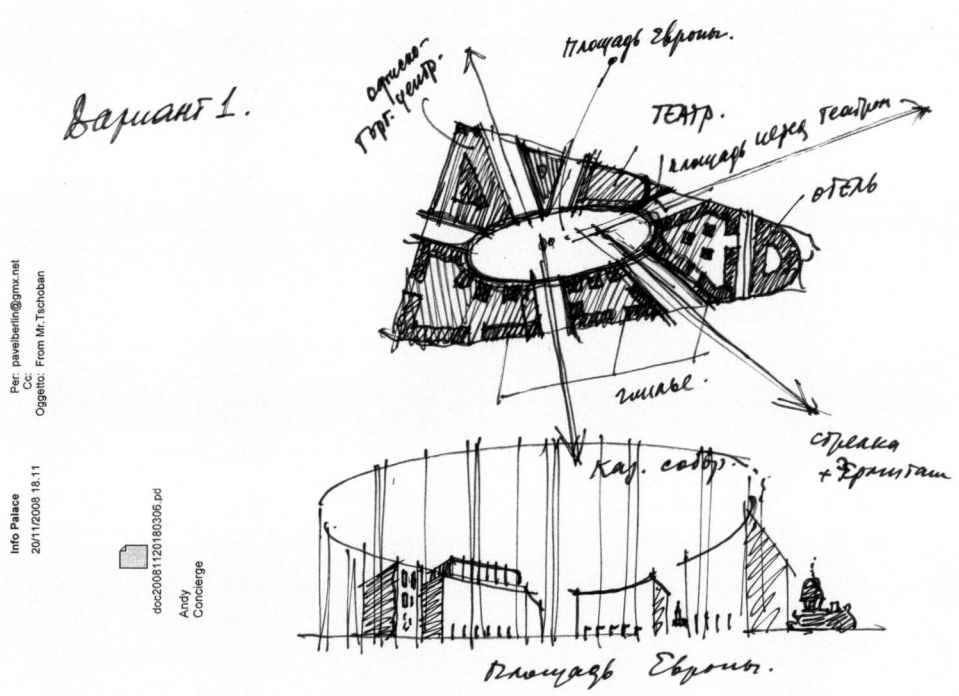

SKETCH FOR FEDERATION COMPLEX, MOSCOW, FINELINER ON PAPER, 2005, ARCHIVE TCHOBAN VOSS ARCHITEKTEN

SKETCH FOR FEDERATION COMPLEX, MOSCOW, FINELINER ON PAPER, 2005,
ARCHIVE TCHOBAN VOSS ARCHITEKTEN

The car seems to play a major part in your day-to-day professional life.

My car has become a kind of refuge for me and, in a manner of speaking, my own private office. Whenever my driver picks me up from an appointment or from the airport after I've been on a trip, he brings a pile of mail with him, and I usually manage to work through it before we arrive at the office or my house. If I don't, I'll stay in the parked car until the last of the letters has been answered. In this way, I'd almost describe myself as obsessive. I try to answer all emails within two hours. After that, I tell my driver how everything has to be distributed and forwarded.

This feeling of having done everything and not needing to take anything with me into the following days is incredibly important for me.

In that moment you are free to think, because you know there is nothing weighing you down and that you've taken care of everything. Of course I know what an unbelievable luxury it is to have a car with a driver, but it's a necessity for me. I used to be a passionate driver myself; I drove a lot, very fast, too, with the music at full blast, always hurrying from one meeting to the next, and then the hunt for a parking space, or the trip to the airport, usually at the last minute, park the car, run to the gate, then slump into the seat. But at some point, when you count the hours you spend doing this, then you realise that it's all lost time, useless and exhausting.

From First Sketch to Finished Building

SKETCHES FOR THE BOOK "ARCHITECTURAL CONTRAST", CHARCOAL ON PAPER, 2015, TCHOBAN FOUNDATION

From First Sketch to Finished Building

NEVSKAYA RATUSHA (NEVSKY CITY HALL), SAINT PETERSBURG, 2016

During our conversations, you have often used the terms consistency, structure and logic. Your work is characterised by these things on all levels: in the design process, in preparing a presentation as well as in the presentation itself, in the realisation of your projects, etc. You organise all your work processes in detail – and those of your employees. What's your motivation for this?

In the course of a day, I have to negotiate a number of different tasks that are normally planned very precisely. I attach a great value to this, because the same also applies here: leave as little to chance as possible. This kind of consistency, the clear processes, I've always been like this somehow. It's my way of structuring myself, my life and my work. I think it's imperative to not lose this orderliness in the overall design process. In our profession it's very, very easy to lose track of things quickly if you don't establish these structures for yourself. I'm quite sure of that. I try to keep the problem of what I see as lost time to a minimum by the structure I give to my work. The time that I gain through doing this is vital for me. It's alarming how much lost time accumulates in the course of a day alone. Time you squander without even being aware of it. I think you should at least lose it consciously, for example by watching a stupid series on your tablet or sitting in front of the television. That's fine. I prefer to use this time to let my thoughts run free, to reflect on my work as an architect or to draw. Time is precious, you shouldn't waste it. At the risk of sounding paradoxical: the time I gain in this way is an indispensable part of my architectural practice.

WATER SPORTS PALACE, KAZAN, 2012

Everything Begins with the City

Part 2

KRISTIN FEIREISS AND SERGEI TCHOBAN IN CONVERSATION

In our first conversation we talked about the design process, about your way of working and your creative and conceptual approach to the task at hand. This conversation will focus on the many different aspects of the city: cultural, social, economic, environmental and above all architectural. Discussing this seems to me to be of particular importance, because it forms the starting point of your thinking and practice as an architect – from entire building ensembles down to the smallest details. Let's begin with the first place that you consciously experienced: Saint Petersburg, where you were born. I would like to know more about your childhood and your youth, especially in relation to your personal development and your choice of career. What fascinated you as a child, what scared you and what piqued your curiosity?

The most important aspect of my childhood was alternating between two apartments and thus two worlds. One of these apartments was in the city centre, which is where my grandparents lived; the other, where my parents lived, was in a new housing development. This apartment was smaller but very light, and quite modern for the time. Before I went to school, I stayed with my parents at the weekend and with my grandparents during the week. The contrast between these two residential and living environments was somehow a bit frightening for me. The housing development was in beautiful surroundings with lots of trees and a small pond called the Silver Pool. You could swim in it in summer and in winter you could ice skate on it, or even go skiing in the hills nearby. The apartments here were highly sought-after. They belonged to a cooperative, today you might call it a co-housing group – of which there are currently quite a lot of in Berlin.

Everything Begins with the City

When did your parents move into that apartment?

It must have been the late 1960s. I was four or five years old; I still remember it well. And I can still remember how I felt about the huge contrast that I perceived between those two worlds.

You've described the world of your parents' apartment; what about that of your grandparents'?

Even as a young child, I was incredibly fascinated by the historical city centre, which is where my grandparents lived – in Dmitrovsky Lane. It's still called that today. It's a typical inner-city area of Saint Petersburg, and I still stay in that apartment when I visit. When I was young, a tram line operated along this narrow lane, which was only about 12 to 14 metres wide. It was really cramped, and I can remember what an unbelievable racket the tram used to make. Nevertheless, or maybe precisely because of this, it was an atmosphere that intrigued me: the different façades of the old houses with their sculptural decoration, the dour colours of the flaking plasterwork, the smells; all of this was extremely exciting for me. There was also a communal inner yard, a typical Saint Petersburg courtyard, bordered to the rear by a theatre. From the kitchen window of my grandparents' apartment I could see the actors in their costumes. It was an enchanting, mysterious world to me. But it probably wasn't a nice place to live for my grandparents. There was a musty smell in the stairwell, which always seemed to be a little damp; the stairs were made of cold, heavy stone slabs, and of course it didn't have a lift. The third floor is not that far up for a small child, but it was for my grandmother carrying things up and down the stairs every day. In my parents' apartment, on the other hand, everything was different, more modern. Needless to say, there was a lift, as well as a central waste disposal chute. Everything was light and pleasant,

THE APARTMENT OF SERGEI TCHOBAN, SAINT PETERSBURG, 2017

Everything Begins with the City

PARK IN LENINGRAD WITH VIEW ON THE CHURCH OF THE SAVIOR ON BLOOD, INK, WHITE HIGHLIGHTS, PAPER, 1979, TCHOBAN FOUNDATION

but it was a bit jarring for me that this environment, which was actually quite luxurious, somehow didn't seem to work. I was always very happy when my mother took me to my grandparents during the week. When my grandmother looked after me it always felt like a great party.

When did this situation change?

When my parents and my grandmother swapped apartments. My grandfather was no longer alive at that point, so my grandmother moved to the greenery of the outskirts. Everything seemed perfect, yet nothing was perfect. No one wants to be exiled. When I think about it all these years later, I find it quite staggering – or perhaps not – that one can so accurately pinpoint what one considers to be a good environment to live in, and that "perfection" doesn't seem to be a decisive factor.

What was – and is – the decisive factor for you? Can you describe it?

As I said, it certainly is not perfection; it's more the spatial experience. Today I would call it the quality of the space. I had a similar, very intensive experience many years later, I think it was 1984, when I was studying at the Russian Academy of Arts in Saint Petersburg. A fellow student and I were asked if we could give private art lessons to the children of two Saint Petersburg families. That was something special for us. We were really interested in the job, and it didn't involve much work. One of the families lived in an old residential area of a typical Saint Petersburg district, right next to the Moskovsky railway station. The other family lived in a new residential development on the outskirts of the city, which had what was considered to be a very progressive urban structure at the time, with expansive, open courtyards and play areas between the apartment blocks.

CORNER GARDEN IN DMITROVSKY ALLEY, LENINGRAD, CHARCOAL ON PAPER, 1978,
TCHOBAN FOUNDATION

WINTER CANAL IN LENINGRAD, INK, CHARCOAL ON PAPER, 1978,
TCHOBAN FOUNDATION

BACKYARD IN SAINT PETERSBURG, CHARCOAL ON PAPER, 2010, TCHOBAN FOUNDATION

VIEW ON THE BELL TOWER OF ST VLADIMIR'S CATHEDRAL IN SAINT PETERSBURG,
CHARCOAL ON PAPER, 2010, TCHOBAN FOUNDATION

What were these private lessons like, and how does this answer my question about what constitutes a good environment to live in?

I'll come back to that. First let's focus on the art lessons. We initially began by doing still lifes or choosing things from the natural world that the children could draw: a tree, a plant, an animal. But when we asked them to draw something unspecified and let their imaginations run free, we saw something quite astonishing. The children who lived in the old residential area chose to paint imaginary golden animals and friendly fairy-tale characters, whereas the children from the new housing estate drew war scenes. They were terrifying images of burning houses and soldiers stumbling over each other, and it didn't make a difference whether our students were boys or girls. We were actually shocked by these different choices of motif. At the time we thought the explanation lay in the surroundings that the children grew up in: one set of children lived in an environment that while not perfect, was manageable in size and familiar, with its inner yards and narrow streets in which they could imagine their own little worlds; the other lived in what was to them a huge, unintelligible, anonymous no-man's land through which they had to navigate to get to the entrance of their block. There were probably gangs in the neighbourhood too, who they felt threatened by and who they had to defend themselves from. I know this from the time I lived in my parents' apartment, and I remember the fear of being attacked when I was walking through the parks adjacent to the new housing developments in the evening. At the time, our attempts to find explanations were rather intuitive. Looking at it today, I consider this behaviour to be a consequence of open urban structures, as they are sometimes so positively referred to, in which urban space dissolves, as it were, dissipating along with the disappearance of social cohesion. In addition to this, there are the loveless construction techniques used in these developments

BACKYARD IN LENINGRAD, WATERCOLOUR, PENCIL, PAPER, 1978, TCHOBAN FOUNDATION

Everything Begins with the City

VIEW ON SAINT ISAAC'S CATHEDRAL, LENINGRAD, INK ON PAPER, 1978,
TCHOBAN FOUNDATION

which, despite all their technical innovations, were implemented due to a lack of money and time. This has grave consequences.

From the 1950s onwards, the controversial American psychoanalyst and child psychologist Bruno Bettelheim, who died in 1990, examined the mental and emotional development of children in relation to the built environment. This included investigating the relationship between problematic, often aggressive behaviour of children and young people and the anonymous residential blocks that they lived in. Bettelheim factored in the visual deficiencies of such housing estates as well as other questions, for example whether living on a higher floor exaggerated their problematic behaviour. The key insights of his investigation concerned the anonymity of the surroundings, the lack of identification with the living environment, a shortage of places where residents could come into contact with each other, and the inhospitable semi-public areas – such as long, narrow, poorly lit corridors and stairwells – where young people's ill-being and aggression were given free rein in the form of vandalism and graffiti. For Bettelheim, such living models were among the main causes of aggression and vandalism in children and young people.

I define the phenomenon you are describing there with the word "loveless", a term used by the distinguished Russian film director Andrey Zvyagintsev. *Loveless* is also the name of his recent beautifully sombre, poetically realistic film. I was deeply impressed by it. I have never before seen a film in which architecture is given such an explanatory power. You find this "lovelessness" everywhere in our cities, it's never far away. The film reflects the tragic story of a family in the bleak environment around them, their emotions conveyed through images of the city and the apartment they live in. It shows the walls of the houses that the child walks past, a child that ultimately goes missing owing to the inattentiveness and lovelessness of his self-absorbed parents; or walls the parents walk alongside when they are searching for their lost child. In contrast, although it is mostly raining or snowing in the film, nature is depicted in a very tender way: a row of leafless trees and its reflection in the water, for example.

There is a tension in the absurd contrast between nature and the dismal uniformity of the built environment, the dreary monotony of daily life.

The inhabitants of this world are deadened and indifferent, and not even the search for and eventual loss of a child can rouse them from this state. For me, this is the consequence of absolute lovelessness: no one is there for anyone else, there is nowhere to feel at home. The film emphasises this in the unsightly remains of a 1970s building complex where the search for the missing child is taking place, and in the monotonous, mass-produced buildings that scatter the environment and convey an unbelievably desolate impression. I see this lovelessness towards people, towards our surroundings, on a small and a large scale; it is something that I try to fight against in everything I do by striving to create a more liveable, loveable environment.

Your sensitivity to your surroundings and your keen sense of what is happening around you, which even manifested itself during your childhood, suggest that you were subject to a strong artistic influence in your parents' household.

I don't think one can really say that. My whole family were scientists. My grandfather on my mother's side was a well-known professor at the Technical University in Saint Petersburg and was the engineer in charge of developing their gas turbine plants. My father was a quantum physicist and a professor at the same university that my grandfather had taught at many years before, and my mother also worked there as an engineer. So there weren't actually any artists in my family, although my parents were always interested in art, especially music. We had a grand piano in our apartment, which everyone played, and my parents were particularly good. They were also both quite good at drawing – and my father even made wall newspapers for me to put up in school.

What did these wall newspapers look like?

Wall newspapers in this form were probably a Soviet invention to get parents to actively participate in their children's lessons. A group of children would be given an assignment by the school, for example to make one of these wall newspapers with the help of their parents. The idea was to report what the class had done over a certain period of time – like a school newspaper but on a single large sheet of paper. It would be made up of texts and drawings, with photos of pupils, teachers, school trips and festivals stuck between them. My father always made them so perfectly and I was immensely proud of them. I would say that my parents had creative talents, they just never realised them. They had other occupations.

Then how did drawing became such a central part of your childhood development? Was there a particular formative experience?

I really enjoyed drawing the houses and streets from my neighbourhood when I was a young boy. In this sense, there

Everything Begins with the City

OVER THE ROOFS OF LENINGRAD, INK ON PAPER, 1979,
TCHOBAN FOUNDATION

was no singular formative experience, but there was a fortunate providence that enabled me to develop further in this direction. My grandmother's sister lived next to an art school, and one day she took in my drawings to show them. This school, the only one of its kind in Saint Petersburg, was considered to be a breeding ground for artists, even if at the time it was for those with a certain point of view – that of realist art, realist painting. That's no longer the case today. The fact that this school accepted me was a defining moment for my professional development and for my life in general, even if I wasn't aware of it at the time.

How old were you at that point?

I started visiting this art school when I was ten years old, I think. In order to be admitted, you had to pass an admission exam in three subjects: free composition, still-life painting and still-life drawing. If you received the grade "good" in all three subjects, you got through. The classes there were very small and consisted of just 12 to 15 pupils. That was quite extraordinary when compared to normal schools, where 40 to 45 pupils in a class was the norm.

The teachers at the school must have recognised your talent. Perhaps they were hoping you would become a famous painter. But then again you did become a famous architect.

I think the teachers at the school, who would have seen that my drawings mostly featured architecture, knew before I did that fine art wasn't for me. I was really searching for something that interested and inspired me, and my teachers encouraged me to take this route.

THE CHURCH OF ST JOHN THE BAPTIST ON OP
CHALK, PEN

SLAV'S COURT IN NOVGOROD, 1979, TCHOBAN FOUNDATION

CHURCH OF THE TRANSFIGURATION OF THE SAVIOR ON ILIN STREET IN NOVGOROD, CHALK, PENCIL ON PAPER, 1979, TCHOBAN FOUNDATION

CITY WINDOW, WATERCOLOUR, PASTEL, PENCIL ON PAPER, 2009,
TCHOBAN FOUNDATION

CITY WINDOW, WATERCOLOUR, PASTEL, PENCIL ON PAPER, 2009,
TCHOBAN FOUNDATION

WHAT WE SEE AND WHAT WE DESIGN, RED CHALK AND CHARCOAL ON PAPER, 2016, TCHOBAN FOUNDATION

Everything Begins with the City

KRONPRINZENGÄRTEN, BERLIN, 2017

Was there a specific moment when it became clear to you that you wanted to be an architect and that this profession was the only choice for you, even though it entailed much more than just being able to produce elaborate drawings?

Yes, there was. It was a long road between having a passion for drawing and being an architect responsible for contributing to the make-up of the built environment. Along this long road, however, there were two very definite experiences. The first was after I had completed year 8, at the beginning of my teens. It was during a work experience placement in which I had to paint motifs of the historical centre of Saint Petersburg in watercolours. I was really fascinated by the urban environment, the streetscapes, and how sometimes, between the houses, a famous building would appear and eclipse everything else in terms of beauty of expressiveness, or how a ruin within a block of houses affected me like a sore on the city. This period of work experience was incredibly important for me and it inspired me to draw houses and three-dimensional scenes, and also later to become an architect.

The second experience was towards the end of my time at school, when, because of my interest in old Russian architecture, I visited many old Russian cities. I especially loved the medieval Hanseatic city of Novgorod, a former meeting point of Russian and Hanseatic culture, with its richly decorated two-storey merchant houses, historical church square and many impressive small churches that were built between the 12th and 15th centuries. Yes, these were the two pivotal experiences from my childhood and my youth.

How did it progress from there?

The next step on my professional journey was the Russian Academy of Arts in Saint Petersburg. To this day, I've still never experienced such an incredible sequence of rooms as in this majestic building. On entering the academy, you are overwhelmed by the grand, yet harmonious spectacle of the entrance hall, from which the unbelievably high, narrow and contrast-rich corridors branch off. It had a quite exceptional ambience, which I also experienced to some extent in the Accademia di Belle Arti di Brera in Milan. And the stunning library! It reminded me of an oversized wooden casket. I think the building itself was maybe the most memorable experience of my studies, even more so than my teachers.

So far, we have talked about your personal development and what influenced and reinforced your desire to become an architect, but what about the people you build for, who will live or work in your buildings, who will visit your museums, cultural centres, cinemas and schools? What role do people play in your architecture?

    I don't actually see myself as an idealist who can solve society's problems. I never had this conception of the profession I chose, but that doesn't necessarily mean, however, that the residents, the users of my buildings, aren't the focus of all I do and how I go about it. I want to define spaces that, in my opinion, function on a human scale. With each individual project I seriously strive to create spatial solutions that contribute to improving quality of life, to create spaces that people feel good in, that don't constrict them, in which they can evolve or seek refuge. And even my starting point is what I myself would like; this is obviously different for every single person – every family, every office, every shop owner – and that's what you need to find out through dialogue. I first test out spatial situations on myself and see how they affect me, see what I like and what bothers me, and then exchange experiences with the people I'm building for. I try to find out their expectations and requirements, assess them together, make suggestions, see how they react and then try to arrive at the right solution together. I think that my answer to your question about the role people play in what I do is: listening carefully and taking their needs seriously, but also incorporating my own experience as an architect to design an engaging spatial arrangement that fits their needs.

I don't think I know another contemporary architect who has such a rigorous – I almost want to say existential – approach to urban space as you, and someone who defines every one of his buildings through its role in the urban landscape. I'd like to return to something you said about your childhood, about the different residential and living situations of your parents and your grandparents. Your descriptions give the impression that something crucial was lost. What do you feel is missing in the cities of today? And what role does architecture play in this?

It's not just about what I personally miss and how I experience the city.

It's about how people act in public spaces: which ones give them a sense of well-being, which inspire them, which ones scare them, which ones they avoid, and whether the person walking alongside me down the street perceives the same thing I do.

In every city, in every region that I spend any amount of time in, I try to figure this out. I take a lot of pictures of details, of street scenes featuring people, so I can later reflect on what kind of impression a certain situation had on me and whether I can learn something from it.

FANTASY TO ETCHINGS BY PIRANESI, SEPIA INK, WATERCOLOUR AND GRAPHITE ON PAPER, 2017,
TCHOBAN FOUNDATION

THE URBAN LAYERS 4, WATERCOLOUR, INK, PAPER, 2014, TCHOBAN FOUNDATION

Everything Begins with the City

MODERNISTIC CITY, REMINISCENCE OF IRAN, PASTEL, CHARCOAL ON PAPER, 2016,
TCHOBAN FOUNDATION

You've given a very vivid description of how you perceive the city, but what specifically do you find to be lacking in today's cities?

The more I think about it, the more apparent it becomes to me that there are two things that I find lacking in most cities today. The first is a spatial composition, a spatial mise en scène of the city in which the houses and open spaces stand in a clearly defined relationship to one another, creating interesting, multifaceted urban contexts. An urban environment that is arranged like a free surface on which individual objects have been placed, on the other hand, I refer to as a "city of objects" – and I don't mean it in a positive way. It's like the buildings are sculptures located in a large park. But houses aren't sculptures; people live inside them, and as a result of this spatial arbitrariness they inevitably lose contact with each other. In my opinion, this is a totally incorrect approach. I like vistas of streets and squares, urban spaces of different scales, ones that become wider and narrower again, sometimes filled with shadows, sometimes with light. And through my architecture and city planning I want to give back these spatial experiences to people; spatial experiences that underwent a break with classic modernism. At some point while reflecting on the urban environment, I asked myself: can modernism fit in? Does it even have the capacity to be assimilated? And I concluded that modernism, with its distinct architectural language, that we all love so dearly, this avant-garde, which we view as modern and progressive, can do many things, but one thing it cannot do is fit in. For that reason, modernism is much more compelling in the form of prominent individual buildings and less convincing in terms of urban planning. I don't think I have to go into this any deeper right now. Everyone who has anything to do with city planning knows about this development.

Everything Begins with the City

You have some heavyweight allies in your critique of modernism, but it has also a large number of admirers and followers. One of modernism's most outstanding contemporary proponents is the Brazilian architect Paulo Mendes de Rocha, who won the Pritzker Prize in 2006 and the "Golden Lion" at the Architecture Biennale in Venice in 2016. In contrast to the significance that you ascribe to ornamentation in everyday architecture, Mendes has been quoted as saying: "I'm not afraid of clarity, even poverty, as only then can you recognise what is necessary."

That's a great quote! The clarity and poverty of modernism allows us to see what is necessary, or, to put it more accurately, what is lacking. If a modernist building has an expressive form, then it's surely not lacking anything. These are the beacons of modernism, and if they are renovated regularly enough, they will remain with us in this form for a long time. But, as is the case with the so-called background architecture of the modernist age, and that's the majority of the building stock, if their form is "square, practical, good", then this no longer holds true, and the poverty of their façades immediately reveals what they need: a richer structuring of their exteriors, so they can age in a "self-respecting" manner and not pitilessly, sporting the unsightly yet very visible traces of time. This background architecture, which we have discussed again and again in our conversations, has to protect itself with a specific, appealing appearance and become a kind of protected entity in itself. Otherwise, if it ages badly, no one will pay for the expensive renovations, and these buildings will simply be torn down without a second thought. This is happening everywhere, and with it there is a mass disappearance of the architecture from the 1950s to 1980s. As an approach, it is neither energy efficient nor historically sensitive. But if we don't challenge this way of thinking today, that is exactly what will happen to such buildings.

Besides modernist urban planning, you are concerned with the quality of the exterior surfaces and façades.

I miss the quality of the surface materials and how they feel, the meaning of the materials chosen, the intricacy of the ornamentation – this also experienced a break during modernism. It's no wonder – indeed, it's only logical – that residents of such cities no longer have any interest in looking at these monotone façades; there isn't a single detail to hold one's gaze.

Your book 30:70. Architecture as a Balancing Act, *published in 2017, which you wrote together with the Russian architecture historian Vladimir Sedov, is an analysis of 2,500 years of architectural history. In it you demonstrate what contemporary architecture needs to bear in mind in order to achieve a harmonious relationship between architectural monuments and the many structures that surround them. You put forward the hypothesis that contemporary architecture is divided into statement architecture and everyday architecture. For me, in addition to its academic approach, the book is interesting because it also offers a context in which to understand you and your work as an architect and city planner. What is the fundamental message of this architectural survey?*

First of all, it's about the fact that every era leaves behind celebrated, symbolic structures that are testaments to the architecture and culture of the respective epoch and country. The crucial difference between then and now is that throughout the ages, this everyday architecture – that is to say the vast majority of the buildings within the urban environment – has been treated in a completely different way to how it is today.

Everything Begins with the City

"30:70. ARCHITECTURE AS A BALANCING ACT",
DOM PUBLISHERS, BERLIN, 2017

But in every era, the prominent, monumental buildings were built for the elite while the normal buildings were for the general population. In what way is this different to today?

That's true, it's always been the case that everyday architecture has been simpler than monumental architecture. But it has never been the case that this background architecture, as we also call it, has been constructed in such a sparse, loveless way, without any regard to the sculptural diversity of the façades, as it is today. In the past, indeed throughout the centuries, a small, everyday structure was built according to the same principles as a large, representative building. So if a representative building had a porticus, a colonnade, then an everyday building would also have had one; and if a monumental building featured a structuring of the different storeys, a normal building would have had this too. The main difference was in the scale and the more grandiose, higher quality artistry, and often the value of the materials used. In our book, we refer to this as the "harmony of analogies", which means that the simple building and the representative building were designed analogously. This in turn gave rise to the term "contrast harmony" or the "harmony of contrasts".

Can you give me an example of a harmony of analogies?

Paris or Barcelona come to mind. They are both cities that inspire me. Of course, people visit Paris to see Notre Dame, the Louvre and many other places of interest, but before you get to the Louvre, you have to walk through streets that are just as fascinating and captivating, because they form the true texture of the city. And if you do then visit a major building, the Louvre for instance, you will notice that this representative building has a similar texture to the everyday architecture, only it is on a larger scale and the design is much richer. As these exterior surfaces were constructed in the same way, with a similar density and a similar precision, it creates a great harmony, a uniformity between the different building types. The decisive factor is that a similar amount of attention went

Rather than seeing the contrast and the difference of the dimensions and forms, you see the uniformity of the texture that holds the ensemble together.

into the execution of the everyday architecture as went into the monumental architecture. This is a principle that has been completely lost in modern times. Vladimir and I chose the analogy of the diamond ring. The diamond represents the monumental building and the ring the more modest buildings in which it is set. It is crucial that this ring isn't made of tin, comparable to the loveless, cheaply produced background architecture, but of a much nobler metal – also in a figurative sense.

Does that mean that the majority of the everyday architecture produced in recent decades is of no value?

That's a drastic way of expressing it, but yes, you could say that. The fact that the density of the surface structures that previously unified representative and everyday architecture has been lost, substituted by cheap, plain surfaces without structure and texture, means that this ring – to stay with the analogy – is no longer made of gold but of tin and is thus worthless.

What are the consequences of this development you describe?

That everyday architecture, the normal buildings, are, so to speak, left to fend for themselves and have to somehow safeguard themselves against the ageing process. In a sense, they are naked and unloved. This lovelessness towards the surface materials and the sculptural form – particularly in the detail – can be seen in the majority of everyday buildings, the so-called background architecture, of the last 50 or 60 years. Nowadays, the texture of the buildings can no longer be unified, because the landmark buildings, with their expressive formal language, no longer need this texture as they stand in contrast to their surroundings. Their language is now different, expressive, they are characterised by unusual forms and materials.

This kind of architecture doesn't fit into the surroundings, it forms a counterpoint, a new type of harmony: the harmony of contrasts.

This means that the background architecture, almost exclusively a simple, cubic form without any interesting surface detail, needs to be given a rich texture once again, so that the ring of tin in which the newly cut diamond is set is turned back into gold.

Is contemporary building policy compatible with your theory of the harmony of contrasts?

Today, the most pressing question when I or any other architect presents their design to the relevant architectural advisory board is: "Does your building fit into the surroundings?" This is precisely defined in §34 of the German Building Law.

ACKERSTRASSE 29, BERLIN, 2016

THE WHITE, BERLIN, 2016

VIEW FROM THE WATERSIDE PROMENADE OF THE RIVER SPREE

BOXHAGENER STRASSE, BERLIN, 2018

BUSINESS HOUSE LANGENZIPEN, SAINT PETERSBURG, 2006

CUBIX CINESTAR ALEXANDERPLATZ, BERLIN, 2001

Everything Begins with the City

ZUEV WORKERS' CLUB, CHARCOAL ON PAPER, 2016, TCHOBAN FOUNDATION

That sounds reasonable. But is it also what you believe, what you are aiming for?

No, it's not. I'll have to explain a bit more to illustrate my position. I frequently find myself in both roles: as a member of architectural advisory committees and as an architect defending his design. Again I find that the criterion of whether a building fits into the surroundings is often the decisive factor in the decision-making process. It's not about preventing prominent architecture, it's about affording a higher status to everyday architecture. I am convinced of this, and I've tried to elucidate it using the "harmony of contrasts" theory: one shouldn't be scared of buildings that may be contentious within their settings, as long as it's high-quality architecture. We should, however, be fearful of the fact that the value of the background architecture, which makes up the vast majority of the urban environment, is not being raised. We need to shift our focus onto this, and it is the responsibility of every individual architect to contribute towards increasing the quality of everyday architecture.

I want to come back to your position on modernism and your criticism that early modernism, with its demonstrative architectural language, was unable to communicate with the historical surroundings in any way. This criticism, however, doesn't extend to the Russian modernists; you rather suggest that they had already set out on the path of what you refer to as the "harmony of contrasts".

Yes, that's right, Russian modernist architects did indeed introduce the idea of the harmony of contrasts in Russia in the 1920s. They were quite different from Le Corbusier, for example, whose Plan Voisin envisaged the demolition of an entire district right up to the Louvre in Paris.

WINE HOUSE RESIDENTIAL COMPLEX, MOSCOW, 2017

Everything Begins with the City

MELNIKOV HOUSE IN MOSCOW, CHALK ON PAPER, 2016, PETER COOK COLLECTION

In Le Corbusier's opinion, the old city had outlived its usefulness and needed to be replaced with a new one in which, by building in a vertical direction, open spaces and green areas would be created. This radical modernist idea literally placed itself above everything else. The Russian modernists, however, experimented with a completely different approach. When the capital was relocated from Saint Petersburg to Moscow in 1918, Moscow was still quite a provincial city with a very fragmented structure. The architects of this time, the Constructivists, integrated their dominant buildings into the surrounding structure in a masterful, contrast-heavy way. Like the Melnikov House or Lissitzky's Wolkenbügel [horizontal skyscrapers] projects by Ivan Leonidov or Ilya Golosov's workers' club. For them and several other Russian modernist architects, it wasn't considered necessary to tear down the historical city for modernism to assert itself, rather that this contrast should be accepted and perceived as an aspect that adds life to the city.

As you have just described it, Russian modernism is an impressive example demonstrating that the problem doesn't lie in separating monumental and everyday architecture, rather, as you have said, that everyday architecture isn't given enough attention and is thus constructed in an inferior manner. But isn't that also a financial issue?

   Certainly. Monumental architecture has always had entirely different means for expressing itself at its disposal – especially financially. Such means and possibilities were never given to background or everyday architecture; nevertheless, the answers being given regarding background architecture today are in no way adequate. It has been totally neglected for some time and has, for the most part, been degraded to the status of investment architecture. This is a huge problem for our cities. To come back to your question, this development has primarily financial reasons. A prominent building will generally be built to a higher quality and subsequently renovated at a later date, as a lot of money has already been invested in it – also because it will usually serve a kind of landmark function for the city. It's different with everyday architecture; the investments in such buildings are much smaller. They need to be able to age well without expensive maintenance and renovations. Carefully choosing materials and surfaces would make a huge contribution towards ensuring this.

Using the paradigm of Moscow in the 1920s and 1930s, you showed in your book how a successful harmony of contrasts can look. To help understand the idea, can you provide a more current example, a paragon of contemporary contrast harmony?

A good example is Frank Gehry's famous Guggenheim Museum in Bilbao, where the adjacent historical building stock didn't just provide a worthy setting for the iconic building. The construction of the Guggenheim Museum also supplied the impetus for the restoration of the surrounding buildings and thus led to an upward revaluation of the whole area.

As referenced in the title of your book, you say the proportion of landmark architecture – for example, the Bilbao Guggenheim Museum – to background architecture in our cities is around 30 to 70. What exactly do you mean by that and what significance does it have?

I want to make it apparent that the built "manifestos", or "statements", in our cities throughout the ages have never exceeded 30 per cent of all buildings. And with 30 per cent I don't mean the number of buildings, that would be much lower, I mean the perceivable building volume. This 30 per cent is in a sustainable

GUGGENHEIM MUSEUM BILBAO, PASTEL, CHARCOAL ON PAPER, 2017, TCHOBAN FOUNDATION

Everything Begins with the City

LUZHNIKI STADIUM, MOSCOW, 2017

urban ratio to the 70 per cent that is made up by background architecture. However, there is a widespread inclination among contractors – and unfortunately also architects – to make each normal building, be it a residential building or an office block, into an architectural monument. You get the impression that almost every instance of everyday architecture now needs to look like a built manifesto. That's the wrong approach, and I see it as my task to keep bringing attention to this. The 70 per cent of everyday architecture shouldn't be characterised by extravagance; it should primarily satisfy its function as background architecture but, and this is my central message, be of a higher quality – in the surfaces of its façade, in its texture and in its materials. That's what needs to change.

But, first and foremost, you are an architect. What is your personal strategy in trying to overcome this perceived impasse of neglected everyday architecture, to which you consciously dedicate a great deal of your work?

That's an interesting question, and perhaps the most pressing one in this context. Above all, there needs to be an increased amount of work and research carried out on new building technologies, because one of the main problems today is with combined walls and hung curtain façades. This is a little technical, but important for a general understanding. In normal buildings, these combined walls predominantly consist of a thin, mounted façade layer that is hung from the thermal insulating material, which to me is the completely wrong approach. In between there is a kind of supporting structure on which these thin layers are hung, be it plates of metal or cement, wallpaper-like stone panels or tiles. This thin layer hangs in front of the load-bearing wall. Interestingly, the eye can subconsciously perceive this set-up. Even if the architect has tried to give the surface an interesting design, with a kind of X-ray vision one can see – and many people have confirmed this – that it isn't real but a cladded wallpaper, a "fake". I like to compare it with someone wearing a mask over their face. The face can age in a dignified manner; the mask can't. At some point, the mask will simply disintegrate, revealing the sweaty face behind – a face that no one recognises.

That's exactly what's happening in construction today. Only when this exterior layer, the mask, decays can you see the affliction behind the "sweaty" thermal insulation, and we're not even close to knowing the full extent of it. It might sound drastic, but it's true, and a fundamental change is needed. In recent years, a few things have been developed to improve the situation. There are now combined walls in which the non-load-bearing layer of the façade is merged with the self-supporting layer of the façade. With my Museum for Architectural Drawing in Berlin, for example, the load-bearing layer is on the outside. And there are also walls that are simultaneously load-bearing and insulating.

A wall without insulation: is that technically possible and legally permissible?

There are now walls that are so insulated in themselves that they don't need extra insulation. That's the future, and it's clear that the construction industry needs to do more work in this direction. I am absolutely sure that if we want to move in the direction of a truly sustainable architecture, in which the buildings don't have to be torn down every 20 years because no one wants to live in them, then the industry must be much more active, and in some fields it already is.

"I am absolutely sure that if we want to move in the direction of a truly sustainable architecture, then the industry must be much more active."

Everything Begins with the City

Do the contractors, developers and the public sector also need to play their part in this? After all, it's about extra costs, and especially in the construction of social housing there are clear parameters as far as costs are concerned. Which arguments can convince the contracting party that such a multifaceted, high-quality, enriching everyday architecture is nevertheless buildable, more sustainable and moreover, with a view towards the future, both practical and necessary?

If you try to explain a certain kind of surface material and procedure to a client, the first question will of course be: "What's it going to cost me?" or, "That's too expensive for this project" and so on. A huge amount of convincing is then necessary and you don't always succeed. The reason is quite obvious: the trend towards an increase in the quality of everyday architecture is happening slowly but steadily, because the decision-makers in the field are becoming more aware of the deficiencies I have spoken of. Luckily, I'm not alone with these ideas: I find myself in the good company of other colleagues and contractors. Over time, it will become increasingly easy to persuade the client that the quality and variety of the surface materials contribute to the sustainability of their buildings, particularly when it comes to everyday architecture. I always explain this with the example of how much you have to paint or clean a surface when it is too smooth. When the façade has a rough surface, if it features ornaments and reliefs, dirt from the city, moisture and everything else that acts upon the building forms a patina on the ornaments and reliefs. The building then ages in a natural way. It will perhaps get wrinkles, but no unsightly staining. In addition, lovingly designed textures and ornamentation on surfaces often prevent the desire for vandalism and reduce the repairs incurred, which leads to more cost-effective upkeep. These are also questions of sustainability, and that's often what actually convinces the client.

We've spoken about new building technologies. What role does craftsmanship play within the constantly changing construction process?

That's an extremely complex question. One can't flippantly say whether craftsmanship, in the original sense of the word, has survived or is coming back. Naturally, the quest for richness in the structure of the surface materials is always a trade-off between artisanship and advanced technology. For me, it's possible that a computer-milled surface can be finished by hand. In my opinion, robots belong to the craftsmen of the future. One shouldn't close oneself off from this eventuality; the methods of work and production will no doubt be different in the future. This also means that things will have to be pre-assembled so that parts can be installed on-site. I think that the interaction between technology and craftsmanship is one of the main challenges in this process.

To close this part of our conversation I would like to return to the architectural analysis you wrote with Sedov, since the conclusions you deduce from it are the foundations on which a great deal of your work is based.

The revaluation of everyday architecture and the development of an architectural language that brings vitality, a richness of surfaces, ornaments and reliefs, as well as the emphasis on haptic details back into the city is indeed central to my work. But it's about much more than that. It's about generally rethinking how we need to develop a more careful, thoughtful approach to our cities, because this is the only possible way to create liveable urban environments that are more compassionate towards their residents. It's a fight against anonymity, uniformity, mediocrity, and the transitory nature of everyday architecture, one that we – architects, city planners, public authorities, private contractors, residents and users – can only win by taking it up together.

"It is a fight against anonymity, uniformity, mediocrity and the transitory nature of everyday architecture that we can only win by taking it up together."

BUSINESS HOUSE LANGENZIPEN, SAINT PETERSBURG, 2006

"THE STORY OF THE BERLIN COURTYARDS", PRESENTATION DRAWING FOR THE PROJECT
"THREE COURTYARDS" IN BERLIN, SEPIA INK ON PAPER, 2018, TCHOBAN FOUNDATION

On Drawing, Collecting and Exhibiting

Part 3

KRISTIN FEIREISS AND SERGEI TCHOBAN IN CONVERSATION

In our first two conversations we spoke about the design process, your approach as an architect and the role the city and the urban context play in your work. As far as the subject of architecture is concerned, we could have left it at those two conversations. This conversation, however, is primarily about Sergei Tchoban the artist, collector and exhibition designer, passions based on your fascination for the medium of architectural drawing and the remarkable things that have stemmed from it over the decades. Firstly, I'd like to return to your childhood in Saint Petersburg, which, as you told us before, had a defining influence on the rest of your life.

I've already mentioned how, as a child, I began drawing my surroundings in Saint Petersburg, albeit often with fantastical embellishments; I would enrich my reality, my personal environment, with depictions from my beloved Pushkin fairy-tale books.

I still have vivid memories of these book illustrations with their fanciful, fantastical, sometimes mystical cities.

It was unbelievably exciting for me to immerse myself in these images, tracing the outlines of the buildings with my finger and deciphering the graphical compositions of these fairy-tale cities.

"The fascination for book illustrations had a great influence on my childhood, and it still remains to this day."

On Drawing, Collecting and Exhibiting

Listening to you reminds me of the children's book Serafin und seine Wundermaschine (Beebo and the Funny Machine) *which tells in imaginative pictures the story of a little kid and his dream house, which is the home of his inspiration and lively fancy. That I have this book still in my mind is because it made me think of my own dreams, my passion and my mission. It sounds like the illustrations in these Pushkin fairy-tale books laid the foundation for your love of this medium.*

That's true. Illustrated children's books are mostly the first thing you come into contact with as a child, before you are later able to go to museums and admire the originals of the great masters. This fascination for book illustrations had a great influence on my childhood, and it still remains to this day. In the last century, there were many distinguished book illustrators who were also artists, such as Ivan Bilibin, for example, who I knew from my Pushkin books. His illustrations were like the folk images of Russian art. In a certain way they are also related to the traditional Japanese drawing and woodblock printing, which influenced me in later years (and which I will come back to later). While reduced on the one hand, Bilibin's images were also very spatial in their structure. Time and again I tried to incorporate these elements in my drawings and aquarelle paintings. I am still fascinated by his extremely precise technique of drawing with ink. Not only could he depict architecture in a very sculptural manner; he also had a way of bringing the figures to life. I was particularly impressed by his magnificent, large-scale works of Cairo's old town, in which he conveyed its dense, highly charged atmosphere in a simple yet unmistakable way.

On Drawing, Collecting and Exhibiting

As an internationally renowned artist, exhibitions of your drawings have been shown in major museums around the world, for example: Sir John Soane's Museum in London, the A+D Architecture and Design Museum in Los Angeles and the Tokyo Art Museum. Whilst some well-known contemporary artists now have their own art collections, I don't know of any who has built up a collection in such a professional way as you – and with this I don't mean collections of their own work. At what point did your fascination for architectural drawing lead you to suddenly say to yourself: "I absolutely have to have that drawing!"?

This also goes back to my childhood. Indeed, my love of drawing and the deep-seated desire to one day start my own collection was formed during this period of my life.

It was the excitement with which I immersed myself in the illustrations of my children's books. Even when I was an art student, and years later, nothing changed. On the contrary, the more intensively one gets to know a subject, the more distinctly one's preferences come to the fore. That's how it was with me and collecting, and it still is. There's Ivan Bilibin, for example, who I've already mentioned, or Alexandre Benois, who, as well as being an outstanding set designer, was a fantastic illustrator and architectural draughtsman.

On Drawing, Collecting and Exhibiting

ALEXANDRE NIKOLAYEVITCH BENOIS, ST. PETER'S BASILICA IN ROME. VIEW ONTO THE ARCO DELLE CAMPANE, WATERCOLOUR, PEN IN BROWN TONE AND GOUACHE AND WHITING OVER A BLACK CHALK PREPARATORY DRAWING, 1903, SERGEI TCHOBAN COLLECTION

OPEN BORDERS. BIENAL INTERNACIONAL DE ARTE CONTEMPORÂNEA DE CURITIBA 2019,
OSCAR NIEMEYER MUSEUM, CURITIBA, 2019

SERGEI TCHOBAN: CONTRASTING HARMONY OF THE CITY, MUSEUM OF ARCHITECTURE, WROCŁAW, 2018

On Drawing, Collecting and Exhibiting

I have to admit that it was only after our previous conversations about collecting over the years that I started thinking about the subject in more depth. Until then, collecting for me was something that everyone does once at a certain point in their lives – and it was of course the same for me. As a small girl I collected shells that I found on the beach and stored them in a precious praline box that belonged to my grandmother; later it was small samples from my uncle's pharmacy that I guarded like treasure – much like my uncle did with his army of tin soldiers, which he only brought out on Sundays. Many people collect things that have a significance at a certain stage of their life, but this has nothing to do with the professional, scholarly form of collecting that you engage in. As the art historian Harriet Roth states in her book Der Anfang der Museumslehre in Deutschland *[The origins of museum theory in Germany], this kind of collecting is first attested to in Samuel Quiccheberg's 16th-century treatise* Inscriptiones vel Tituli Thratri Amplissimi. *In it, he describes the different forms of collecting, from the small, private collections of scholars and special princely collections that were frequently amassed during expeditions, to the first great universal collections which, according to Roth, represented a "macrocosm in a microcosm". In general, these art lovers, scientists, explorers and colonial masters didn't possess this passion for collecting from birth; it evolved from a host of different motivations during the course of their social, cultural, scientific and political lives. You, on the other hand, say that your early childhood preoccupation with drawings never waned as you grew older.*

Let's talk about the artist Sergei Tchoban. It's quite astonishing that you still enter architectural drawing competitions even though, as a world-renowned artist, you really don't need to – quite apart from the fact that your work as an architect doesn't leave you with much free time. What motivates you to do this?

On Drawing, Collecting and Exhibiting

DREAMS OF FROZEN MUSIC – THE ARCHITECTURAL DRAWINGS OF SERGEI TCHOBAN,
TOKYO ART MUSEUM, TOKYO, 2018

I don't have much free time, it's true, but I get great pleasure from taking part in such competitions. I sometimes ask myself why I do this. One reason is that it's a passion of mine, that's quite obvious, but there's also another reason. I think in this respect I'm like a professional athlete, someone who wants to constantly prove themselves and their ability, and who wants confirmation that they are still at the same level or maybe even a bit better. Taking part in one of these competitions is like being on stage, hearing the public or the jury's reaction to your work. This is very important if you want to stay in shape, but it's not the most important thing.

It's simply a pleasure for me to draw real architectural situations as well as visions I have in my head.

The recurring motifs in your artistic works, such as historical buildings and urban scenes, clearly indicate that you like to draw – and draw a lot – while you are travelling. Why?

The reason I like to draw while I'm travelling is because it fascinates me to regularly experience historical buildings and urban contexts that, in my opinion, warrant a drawing. Sometimes I come across historical or contemporary urban spaces that inspire me and make me reflect on my own work as an architect. Later, I often go over my travel sketches and drawings to see which urban situations, façade sequences and surface structures impressed me so much that I wanted to capture them. These insights help me when it comes to reflecting on my own architectural designs.

On Drawing, Collecting and Exhibiting

SERGEI TCHOBAN DRAWING, 2020

"For me a collection must tell a story, or at least a chapter of a story."

Is there a big jump from drawing to collecting?

Where shall I begin? A major reason is undoubtedly that, because I love drawing, I want to collect what I like doing best – besides my work as an architect. Even the "tools of the trade" fascinate me: paper, paintbrushes, pens, paints, and all the rest. There's also the question of the choice of paper, which plays a big role; there's the smell of the wet paper; the paint, which merges with the paper when it is applied; the paintbrush, in its many different thicknesses, and how it changes when it draws up water or paint; there's the moment the pencil or charcoal comes into contact with the paper. This has always affected me, and I'm also sensitive to it in other artists' drawings. I like a lot of artists, and they are all very different. I value images executed in a distinct or highly skilled way.

Another reason is that, in my occupation as an architect, I have learnt that a graphic representation of an architectural situation always serves as a key to understanding the completed building. When I moved to Germany after my studies and wasn't proficient in the German language, I initially began working as an architectural illustrator, translating other architects' designs into drawings. For me, architectural illustration is an excellent intermediary between professionals and lay people. Even though computers can do this nowadays, they don't achieve the expressiveness and explanatory power of a hand-drawn rendering. All these experiences and realisations from my childhood onwards influenced my decision to one day start collecting architectural drawings in a serious way.

AKIHABARA, PASTEL ON BLACK PAPER, 2018, TCHOBAN FOUNDATION

CHIESA DI SAN GIOVANNI BATTISTA IN MATERA, PASTEL ON BLACK PAPER, 2018,
TCHOBAN FOUNDATION

On Drawing, Collecting and Exhibiting

What was the first piece in your collection?

I was in my early thirties when I acquired my first piece. I was a young architect from Saint Petersburg who had just arrived in Hamburg, and I met the well-respected art dealer and collector Herbert Egenolf, an expert in the field of Japanese colour woodblock printing. I bought a print of the first work in Hiroshige's series *One Hundred Famous Views of Edo* from him. Edo, by the way, is the old name for Tokyo. You could say it is a very "architectural" series, one that totally fascinated me. That's how it began. Back then, they weren't first edition prints from this series. It was only years later that I was able to buy a few prints from the very rare original series. With these Japanese colour woodblock prints I fulfilled a childhood dream. They were the first pieces in my collection.

Did you have definite criteria for your choices from the very outset?

Over the years, it became increasingly clear that I was only really interested in representations of architecture, and that was true for all areas of my collection.

The core themes are architectural drawings, perspectives of cities and Japanese colour woodblock prints.

The passion for collecting, and I think you can call it a passion, doesn't happen by chance. The first question was "Where do I start?", as the field of Japanese colour woodblock prints is huge in itself. I then decided on Utagawa Hiroshige. He was one of the last distinguished artists from the famous school for colour woodblock printing in 18th- and 19th-century Japan and is considered the last great master of the ukiyo-e school. His magnificent images inspired Van Gogh and a host of other great artists of the era. Sometimes they even borrowed his motifs. Hiroshige produced several series of colour woodblock prints, such as the one based on Fujiyama, Japan's holy mountain, or of the hiking path that leads through the mountains between Kyoto and Tokyo. I then decided to purchase prints from his final and most famous series, *One Hundred Famous Views of Edo*.

Do you go to auctions yourself?

Occasionally. I had barely heard of the Berlin auction house Bassenge, for example, so I ordered their newest catalogue and immediately found a drawing in it that I was interested in. What a stroke of luck!

What kind of work was it?

It was an Italian set design by Pietro di Gonzaga. I knew straight away that it was an original: it literally radiated.

In mentioning the radiance of an original, you touch on a subject that Walter Benjamin intensively examined in the mid-1930s. In his essay "The Work of Art in the Age of Mechanical Reproduction", he speaks about the "aura of the work of art". As you describe it, this set design by Pietro di Gonzaga definitely had this aura.

Yes, that's how I saw it. I knew about Pietro di Gonzaga's stage designs from my studies of art history, but only from books. At the time I wanted to be able to see them up close and hold them in my hands. The fact that Gonzaga's drawing style seemed very familiar to me was because after my studies I tried, to a certain extent, to evolve in this direction. It's a technique in which you use sepia-brown ink and watercolour – both techniques – together in one drawing.

UTAGAWA HIROSHIGE, AOI SLOPE, OUTSIDE TORANOMON GATE, COLOUR WOODBLOCK, 1857, SERGEI TCHOBAN COLLECTION

UTAGAWA HIROSHIGE, ZŌJŌJI PAGODA AND AKABANE, COLOUR WOODBLOCK, 1857, SERGEI TCHOBAN COLLECTION

On Drawing, Collecting and Exhibiting

Do you always have such luck with your purchases?

Unfortunately not, even though some totally unexpected things have happened in the course of making a purchase. I remember that I also bought another drawing besides this piece, which later proved to be of no real worth. Of course, this happens quite often, because you first have to learn how to screen things and not just immediately buy everything you like when you see it for the first time. I also had another experience that proved to be very enlightening in this context. At a time when I was still unsure whether I was going to exclusively collect original drawings, I bought a veduta by Piranesi in a second-hand bookshop in Hamburg and later compared it to the "serial" version. Contrary to what the seller had claimed, it turned out that it wasn't an original edition. When I went to return it, he said that I could exchange it for something else – and then something quite fortunate happened. I found a wonderful ink drawing in a vitrine in the farthest corner of the shop. The seller handed me the "exchange object" with the words: "We don't know who it's by anyway." Recently, with the help of an art historian, I found this image in the catalogue of a very old Italian collection and ascertained that this drawing was also by Pietro di Gonzaga.

Do you work with art historians?

Yes, regularly. After I had built up the first part of my collection, it was important for me to show it to a specialist within the field. But a consultation only really makes sense if they get an idea of the collector's preferences and proclivities and in which direction they want their collection to develop. I was fortunate to meet a very good adviser. He occasionally criticises me, too, and will perhaps say: "You shouldn't have bought that because it's not in a good enough condition." I still don't always agree with this line of

On Drawing, Collecting and Exhibiting

169

PIETRO DI GOTTARDO GONZAGA, SET DESIGN, PEN, INDIAN INK, WATERCOLOUR,
SECOND HALF OF THE 18TH CENTURY, SERGEI TCHOBAN COLLECTION

argument, however, because for me the drawing of a great artist is always something unique. And then, in the opinion of the expert, it has less of an aura simply because it has faded a little over the years or decades. For me, this is very rarely a reason not to buy such a work. As I said, if you want to build up a great collection, and that's the goal I set myself, then I will happily listen to the advice of experts when I'm making a new acquisition, but I will always make the decision myself.

Is a professional collection defined by its value on the art market?

No, for me it has got absolutely nothing to do with money. It's about the focus of the collection, its concept, its nature and its distinctiveness. I'm not interested in replicating the strategies and ideas of other collectors. For example, if I have a certain artist in mind, then I will also be interested in other artists from the same school. For me a collection must tell a story, or at least a chapter of a story. But, because a story cannot always be told by a single drawing, one should always have at least three or four further works from this same era or school.

There are major international art collectors that have their own, let's say, in-house advisers, maybe even several. Essentially, they won't buy an artwork without a detailed expert opinion that will verify its suitability as an investment. If I understood you correctly, your motivation for collecting differs fundamentally from this approach.

Yes, without a doubt. The financial investment aspect really doesn't apply to me – it's not my goal at all. And as far as advisers go, I can say that I now have quite a keen, well-trained eye myself, which of course is a matter of experience. Recently, I made an interesting discovery regarding a drawing I owned. At first glance it looked pretty good, but when it was on the table in front of me and I was able to study it in peace, it became clear to me that it wasn't an original. Regrettably this was later confirmed, even though I had bought it from a well-respected source. There's a rule of thumb which says you should assume that there's a "counterfeit quota" of around five per cent in any relatively large collection. After I'd developed my first collection of Russian art, my "counterfeit quota" was less than one per cent – more accurately a single piece. In this respect, I think I can safely rely on my own judgement.

So you don't have an adviser?

When it comes to the physical condition of the works, then, as I have said, I frequently need a good adviser, even if I don't listen to him. Occasionally he also goes to auctions on my behalf. This art expert doesn't only advise me, but other collectors, too, and is also an art dealer, so he visits the most important auctions anyway. I would never get around to my work as an architect if I personally went to every auction that I thought looked interesting.

The first step you made on the way to exhibiting architectural drawings was when you designed and erected a small pavilion in the Hackesche Höfe in Berlin, between your office and the Aedes Architecture Forum, where we realised several exhibitions together.

Yes, that's right. It began with this small, spontaneously created, exhibition pavilion, which I designed and realised for Matthias Arndt, now a very well-known gallerist in the contemporary art world. That was in 1999. It was already clear to me at the time that I wanted to open a gallery – or even better a museum – for architectural drawing in Berlin. When Matthias Arndt moved his gallery to a larger space, the pavilion was left empty.

ALEXANDER BRODSKY, EXHIBITION IN THE AEDES EXTENSION PAVILION, BERLIN, 2002

ALEXANDER BRODSKY EXHIBITION

On Drawing, Collecting and Exhibiting

VALERY KOSHLYAKOV, MUSEUM FOR ARCHITECTURAL DRAWING, ADHESIVE TAPE ON PERSPEX, 2016,
TCHOBAN FOUNDATION

It was great that the Aedes Architecture Forum, which was right next door, incorporated the pavilion into its exhibition programme as a kind of annex. The first joint exhibition we put on there was about the very interesting and unconventional Russian artist Alexander Brodsky. We also organised other exhibitions together there, including one of Valery Koshlyakov, an exceptional Russian artist who now lives between Russia and France. Both have a strong connection to ideas of space and architecture.

These small exhibition projects made me realise how interested I was in the conceptualisation and organisation of exhibitions.

But for me, the step from collecting to exhibiting was actually quite a big one.

In the 1990s you also worked closely with Aedes on an exhibition of architectural drawings by members of the American Society of Architectural Illustrators. The variety of architectural themes and the artistic level on display were exemplary. Did this hugely successful exhibition encourage you to exhibit pieces from your collection in other museums?

    The success of this small but wonderfully presented exhibition really encouraged me and eventually inspired me – once my collection had grown a little – to cautiously start exhibiting individual pieces. The exhibition at the Deutsches Architekturmuseum (DAM) in Frankfurt in 2010 was actually dedicated to my own drawings, but I also used the occasion to exhibit some of my key acquisitions with the aim of showing the direction I wanted to go with my collection.

On Drawing, Collecting and Exhibiting

ARCHITECTURAL WORLDS. SERGEI TCHOBAN: DRAFTSMAN AND COLLECTOR, GERMAN ARCHITECTURE MUSEUM (DAM), FRANKFURT AM MAIN, 2010

ARCHITECTURAL WORLDS

This exhibition of yours at the DAM gave visitors the impression they were entering a vault: the walls of the inner room were black, and the space – or more accurately the corridor – around it was white. It was a strong contrast.

This black inner room, the "vault", as you call it, was especially important to me, because there were around ten drawings from my collection on show there. My own drawings in the white corridor surrounding this room provided a frame for it, so to speak. Since then, I have frequently organised exhibitions featuring exhibits from my collection in major museums, including the Cabinet des Dessins Jean Bonna in Paris, the Hermitage in Saint Petersburg, the Pushkin Museum in Moscow and Sir John Soane's Museum in London.

ARCHITECTURAL WORLDS

On Drawing, Collecting and Exhibiting

In 2012, together with Sergey Kuznetsov, Valeria Kashirina and Grigory Revzin, you curated and designed the exhibition i-city/i-land *in the Russian pavilion at the Venice Architecture Biennale. What was your conceptional approach and how did you transform it into the exhibition design?*

For me, developing expressive spaces and the specific character of the interior surfaces formed the basis of the exhibition design, which consisted of two distinct parts featuring entirely different subject matter. The aim of one part of the exhibition was to communicate the concept of the Skolkovo Innovation Center, a district in Moscow, using digital media. We achieved this by converting the rooms – especially the central space – on the upper floor of the pavilion into the form of a dome and decorating its surface with QR codes.

Using the QR codes, visitors were able to retrieve information about the Skolkovo area.

The luminous QR-code surfaces made the space itself seem somehow abstract and futuristic.

In contrast to the upper floor, which presented Skolkovo as a city of the future, the exhibition on the lower level offered visitors a glimpse into the secret cities of the Soviet Union. This space was dark, with small, round, glowing openings in the walls, encouraging visitors to look through the holes of this "imaginary fence" to find previously unknown photographs of these formerly classified cities.

On Drawing, Collecting and Exhibiting

I-CITY / I-LAND, RUSSIAN PAVILION, 13TH VENICE BIENNALE OF ARCHITECTURE, VENICE, 2012

I-CITY / I-LAND

I-CITY / I-LAND

The exhibition, which attracted a great amount of interest from the public and media alike, was awarded a "Special Mention" by the Biennale jury – a great success considering the large number of exhibitions on view. What appeals to you most about designing and organising exhibitions like that one, or others featuring the work of artists or architects?

For me, conceptualising and designing exhibitions has always been an extremely enjoyable, challenging task. I find it similar to designing a stage set, because you have to create a very specific spatial situation. In each of my exhibition designs, I attempt to do justice to the vision of the artists and try to create a world that best frames their work. For the exhibition *Roma Aeterna* at the Tretyakov Gallery in Moscow, in 2016, for example, which featured works from the Vatican Museums, I took inspiration from the traditions of Roman architecture for the exhibition spaces and the surfaces of the walls. Another example is the 2017 exhibition *Giorgio de Chirico. Metaphysical Insights* at the Tretyakov Gallery, in which I practically based the spatial design on de Chirico's images. The public and media interest was overwhelming. I visited the exhibition many times to observe visitors and see the intensity, curiosity and enthusiasm with which they viewed the drawings. These experiences also reinforced my desire to further expand my collection and establish a foundation – the Tchoban Foundation.

ROMA AETERNA. MASTERWORKS OF THE VATICAN PINACOTECA, TRETYAKOV GALLERY, MOSCOW, 2016

GIORGIO DE CHIRICO. METAPHYSICAL INSIGHTS, TRETYAKOV GALLERY, MOSCOW, 2017

GIORGIO DE CHIRICO. METAPHYSICAL INSIGHTS

LA RUSSIA E FATTA A MODO SUO (RUSSIAN PILGRIMAGE), VATICAN PINACOTECA, VATICAN, 2018

JAN VANRIET – LOSING FACE, JEWISH MUSEUM AND TOLERANCE CENTRE, MOSCOW, 2015

JAN VANRIET - LOSING FACE

GARY TATINTSIAN GALLERY, MOSCOW, 2013

THE FORGE OF GREAT ARCHITECTURE. SOVIET COMPETITIONS OF THE 1920S–50S,
SHCHUSEV MUSEUM OF ARCHITECTURE, MOSCOW, 2014

THE FORGE OF GREAT ARCHITECTURE

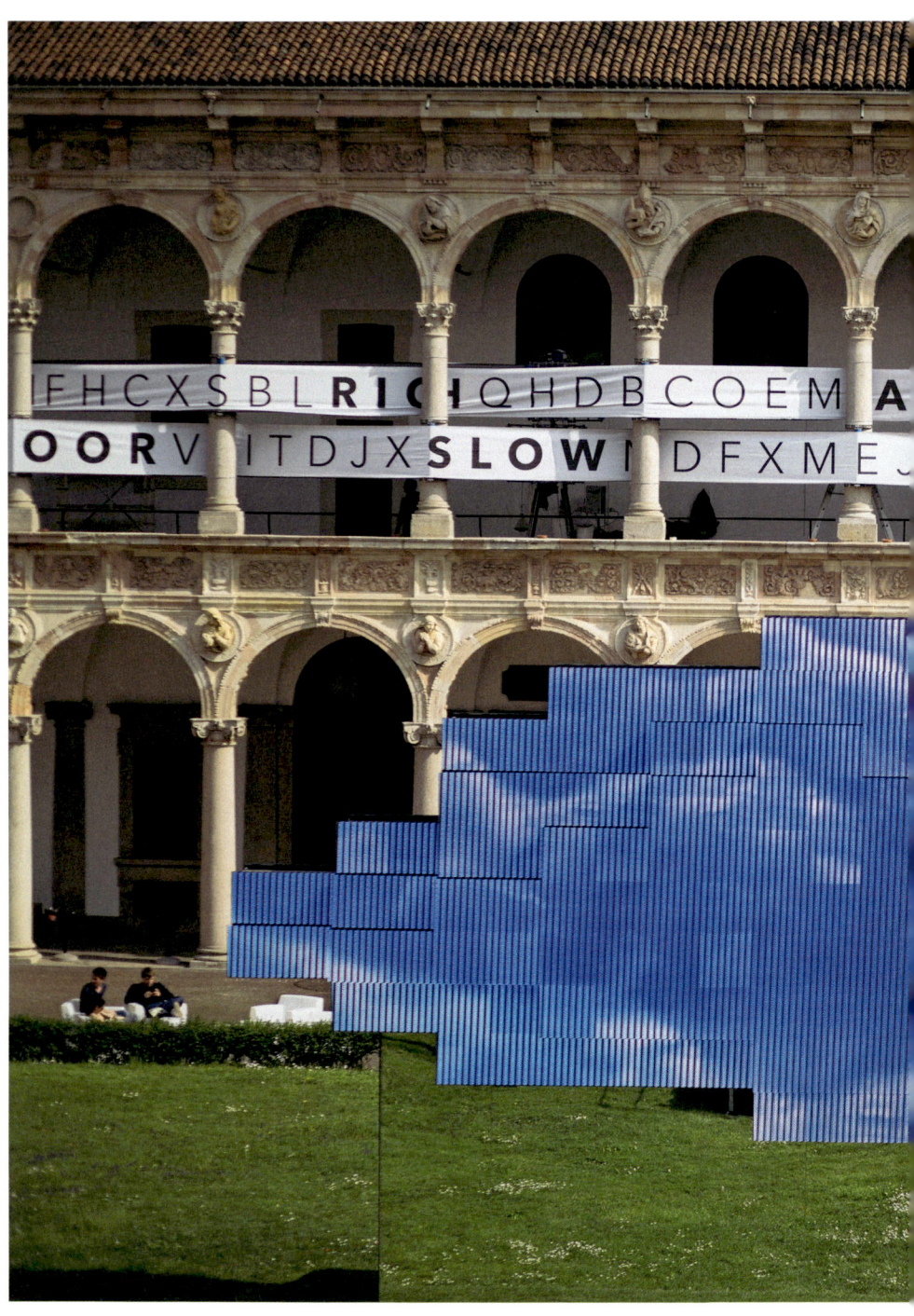

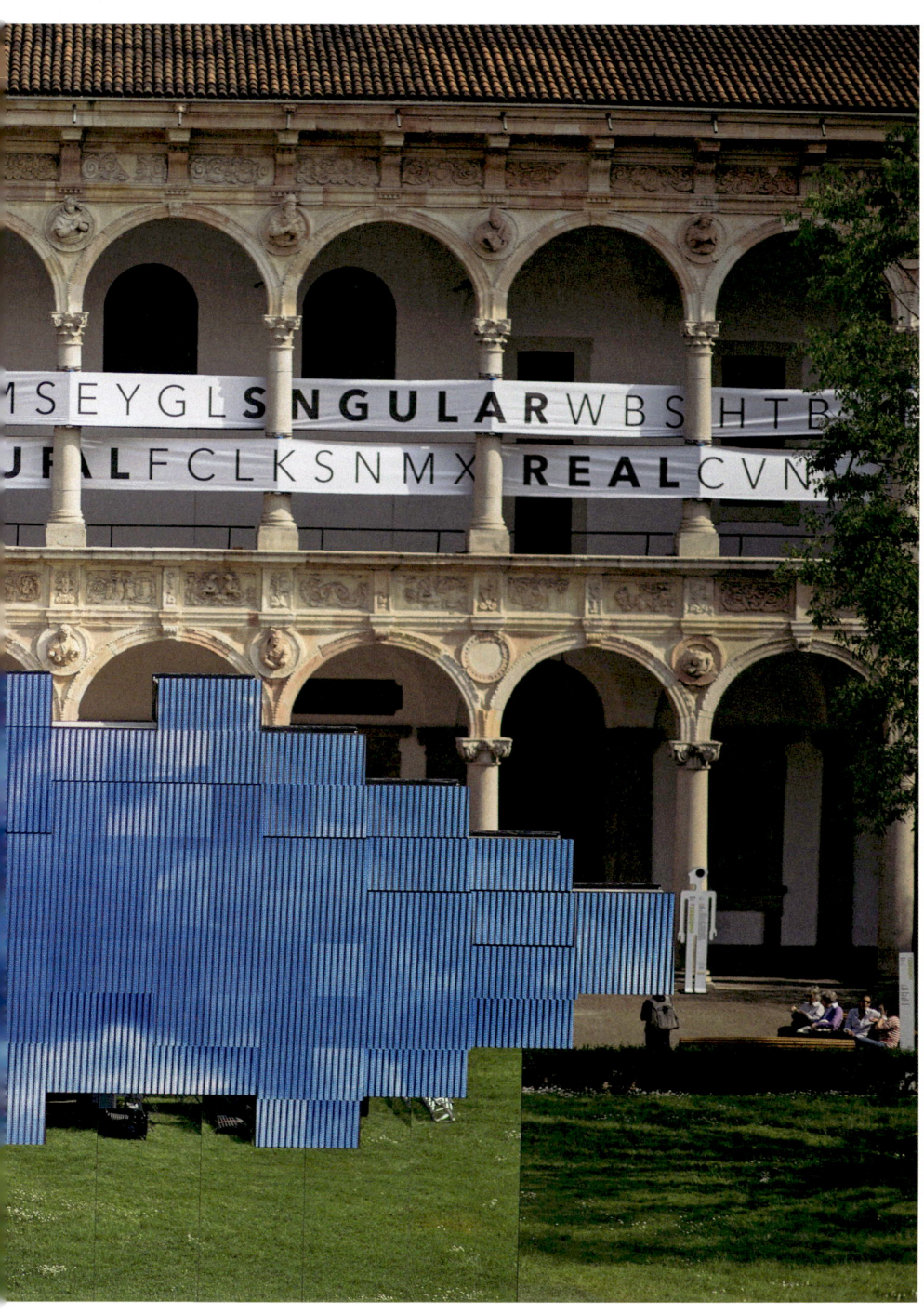

U-CLOUD, EXHIBITION BY INTERNI, MILAN, 2014

LIVING LINE, EXHIBITION BY INTERNI, MILAN, 2015

LIVING LINE

STADTANSICHTEN – PLANSCHRANK MOSKAU / ВЫИД(ЕНИЕ) ГОРОДА – ЧЕРТЕЖНЫЙ АРХИВ МОСКВЫ
(CITYVISION/VIEWS – MOSCOW DRAWING ARCHIVE), IFA-GALERIE, BERLIN, 2004

CITYVISION/VIEWS - MOSCOW DRAWING ARCHIVE

PROJECT SPEECH, MULTIMEDIA ART MUSEUM, MOSCOW, 2016

The Museum for Architectural Drawing

Part 4

KRISTIN FEIREISS AND SERGEI TCHOBAN IN CONVERSATION

The Museum for Architectural Drawing

Now I would like to turn the topic of our discussion towards the Museum for Architectural Drawing, which you founded in 2010 through the Tchoban Foundation, a non-profit organisation created especially for this purpose. This museum is a synthesis of all aspects of your work, your talents, your passions and your visions. It is, without a doubt, your most personal project, one in which you take on many different roles at once: that of founder, architect, collector, artist, curator and exhibition designer. The Museum for Architectural Drawing is also the built expression of your fascination and enthusiasm for architectural drawing, which you wanted to share with other people through this medium. The fact that you also created a building with such architectural impact can be demonstrated by the numerous prizes the museum has won both in Germany and abroad, for example the Chicago Athenaeum Architecture Award, the International Iconic Award and the Architectural Review Award for Emerging Architecture in the UK. In addition to this, the museum was nominated for the European Museum of the Year Award in 2015. It was a long journey to the point where you established the Museum for Architectural Drawing, and the exhibitions you realised before – which we have already discussed – were an instrumental step on this journey.

For the most part, important decisions aren't made spontaneously, they are made up of a series of reflections, experiences and specific, isolated events. I would call them parallel developments. This was how it was with my idea of establishing the Museum for Architectural Drawing. I have already mentioned a few aspects. Another example is the book you and I published together in 2003 called *Hand-Drawn Worlds.* In it we presented architectural

The Museum for Architectural Drawing

HAND-DRAWN WORLDS / HANDGEZEICHNETE WELTEN, KRISTIN FEIREISS (ED.), JOVIS, BERLIN, 2003

drawings by Ken Adam, Zaha Hadid, Lebbeus Woods and many others. The book was a huge success and has sadly been out of print for a while. But for me this was a further affirmation of people's enthusiasm for architectural drawing.

Setting up a museum for architectural drawing doesn't necessarily mean building it yourself. But that is what you did. Indeed, it was the first museum building in your extensive oeuvre. Before we focus on the architecture and contents of the museum, I'd like to talk about a small but very special museum in the Kaluga region of Russia, which you built a few years after realising the Museum for Architectural Drawing: the Museum for Rural Labour. It poetically tells the story of the lives and work of the region's rural population. How did this commission come about?

 Thanks to the initiative of the internationally renowned land-art artist Nikolay Polissky, an art park was gradually created in the Kaluga region – about 220 kilometres south-west of Moscow. Initially, it was only his own magical wooden sculptures – actually small architectural structures – that were exhibited there. Now, the Nikola-Lenivets art park features works by other famous Russian artists and architects. Alexander Brodsky, for example, designed and constructed a very well-known rotunda on the site. And, since 2006, the annual Archstoyanie land art festival has been taking place there, which regularly leads to the creation of new sculptures. In 2014, when I was asked to design and construct a building for the park, there was only one stipulation: you had to be able to enter it. I asked Agniya Sterligova, an architect with whom I had worked many times before, to be co-author and we visited the intended site together, a place surrounded by fields near the village of Zvizzhi.

What were your thoughts about accepting this unusual assignment and choosing to build the Museum for Rural Labour?

It was more of a decision-making process. After examining the location for several days, we decided that we wanted to dedicate a small museum to the rural population. We wanted to express the relationship that these people have to the land through their work and lives. Our aim was to make people aware that their own lives wouldn't be conceivable without this rural "handcraft", as I like to call it. In Russia, this awareness, this tradition, is still very much alive. Our idea was to create a small place with a large impact: a museum in the form of a column, because rural labour is the fundamental pillar of our civilisation. At the same time, the column in its simple form is a major element in the architectural tradition of Russia – from pre-Petrine architecture to constructivist architecture at the beginning of the 20th century.

So, we created a column that you can walk into; an extremely vertical space displaying agricultural equipment from the daily lives of farmers through the ages.

We spent several days gathering each individual piece from people in the surrounding area. In the context of the museum, these erstwhile tools became exhibits and works of art. I have to say that I devoted myself very intensively to this relatively small but fascinating assignment.

The Museum for Architectural Drawing

SKETCH FOR THE MUSEUM FOR RURAL LABOUR, ZVIZZHI, KALUGA, 2015, TCHOBAN FOUNDATION

MUSEUM FOR RURAL LABOUR, ZVIZZHI, KALUGA, 2015

MUSEUM FOR RURAL LABOUR

What type of construction did you decide upon?

The museum consists of a wooden construction clad on the inside and outside with clay – a column made of earth as a symbol of agricultural endeavour. To get inside, visitors have to go through an old, heavy, wooden door, which is incredibly difficult to open, and they have to pick up the key for it from the local municipality. The visitor then enters a circular room 3.2 metres in diameter; their gaze is directed upwards to a skylight at the top of the column, where diffused daylight falls onto the exhibited agricultural tools. Arranged from floor to ceiling in a spiral, they seem to rise into the sky, casting dramatic shadows.

The museum isn't that central, nor is it very easy to get to: where do the visitors come from?

Thanks to the annual art festival, the location doesn't just attract visitors from the surrounding region, but from all over Russia. For many people, visiting this small museum is also quite a special experience. It's like stepping back in time, visiting a secret place. I often find pictures of people on Instagram who have been photographed in front of the museum, including a lot of school children. You can imagine how happy it makes me to see how well it is being received, despite being so far away from any big cities.

Let's move on from the Kaluga region to Moscow and a completely different museum project that you are also involved in: the construction of the new Tretyakov Gallery.

These two projects have proved particularly challenging for me, precisely because they are so different. We just talked about the Museum for Rural Labour, but with the construction of a new building for the Tretyakov Gallery, the most important museum for Russian art, the situation is completely different.

The Museum for Architectural Drawing

SKETCH FOR THE MUSEUM FOR RURAL LABOUR, ZVIZZHI, KALUGA, 2015, TCHOBAN FOUNDATION

INSIDE THE MUSEUM FOR RURAL LABOUR

INSIDE VIEW

The Museum for Architectural Drawing

To begin with, the new building had already been partly built by another architect before the planned façade was rejected by the directors, meaning that a new competition was announced in 2013, which we subsequently won. So, this commission was just for the design of the new façade. We hope the project will be completed in the next couple of years.

Designing the façade of a building that's been built by another architect doesn't sound like a particularly exciting assignment.

That's true in principle, but with such an important museum it can nevertheless prove to be interesting. Even though we're only designing the façade, we've still managed to alter the plasticity and to some extent the structure of the building.

Designing these two museums couldn't have been more different.

That's true, but when I'm commissioned to build a museum, or even just the façade of a museum, it's always a great challenge for me, one that I consciously accept and carry out with all the means at my disposal. Although all projects are important to me, I can say that the Museum for Architectural Drawing and the Museum for Rural Labour in Russia are my most personal ones – they are both very close to my heart.

Where does your fascination for museums come from?

This fascination comes from my home town of Saint Petersburg. As a child, I loved the museums there – especially the Hermitage – and visited them frequently, almost every week. This habit continued when I later studied art and architecture and was able to appreciate the museums and the treasures within them in a more conscious manner.

The Museum for Architectural Drawing

FANTASY ABOUT A MUSEUM FOR ARCHITECTURAL DRAWING, CHARCOAL ON PAPER, 2010, TCHOBAN FOUNDATION

FANTASY ABOUT A MUSEUM FOR ARCHITECTURAL DRAWING, CHARCOAL ON PAPER, 2010, TCHOBAN FOUNDATION

The Museum for Architectural Drawing

Now you have your own prestigious museum with an impressive collection of architectural drawings. I still remember how the museum came about. There was the initial, intensive search for a suitable place, during which you and I visited potential locations in the centre of Berlin together with my Aedes Architecture Forum co-director and partner Hans-Jürgen Commerell. None of them were really suited to your museum concept. This led to your decision to stop looking for an existing building and instead try to find a plot of land to build on yourself.

It was Hans-Jürgen who introduced me to the only suitable place for my museum: a vacant piece of land on the site of the former Pfefferberg brewery, bounded by a firewall on one side. After the Aedes Architecture Forum moved to this location in 2006, and later expanded with the Aedes Network Campus, the foundation was laid for Pfefferberg to become an established cultural hub where, thanks to your mediation, world famous artists such as Ólafur Elíasson and Ai Weiwei set up their studios. Aedes actually played a crucial role in my decision; for decades the Forum has been a magnet for everyone interested in architecture – students, the public and the international architectural community. Our museum, at the entrance to the Pfefferberg site, is located on the way in to it.

The Museum for Architectural Drawing

SITE OF THE FORMER PFEFFERBERG BREWERY, BERLIN, 2010

The Museum for Architectural Drawing

In the more than five years since its opening, the Museum for Architectural Drawing has itself developed into an established address within the local and international art and architecture scene. We'll come back to that later. But first, your foundation – the Tchoban Foundation – had to acquire the plot on the former brewery, a site that dates back to 1841. The starting point of all the projects of yours we've spoken about is the urban context. In the case of your museum, you reacted to the historical surroundings with a contemporary architectural expression. What was your strategy?

I outlined the general strategy in our conversation earlier. Especially when it comes to isolated interventions, contemporary architecture can respond with a high-contrast language and deliberately set a counterpoint to the historical surroundings. We call it the "harmony of contrasts". I came up with a form for the museum at the entrance to the brewery site that, in my opinion, reacts to the wonderful brick façades of the Gründerzeit era in a distinctive, independent way. What's more, the museum is a corner building, which was very important for me given the small overall area of the site and also opened up interesting design possibilities. One of these is the façade of the staggered roof storey, which is accentuated by a glass cube. Another design element is the monolithic façade, whose structure and ornamentation are in keeping with the fragmented nature of the surrounding buildings. From a distance, you initially appreciate the sculptural expressiveness of the museum. It is only when you get closer that you notice the reliefs on the façade.

Can you describe the moment that you made the first sketch for your Museum for Architectural Drawing? What was your approach to the design process for this very special endeavour?

The Museum for Architectural Drawing

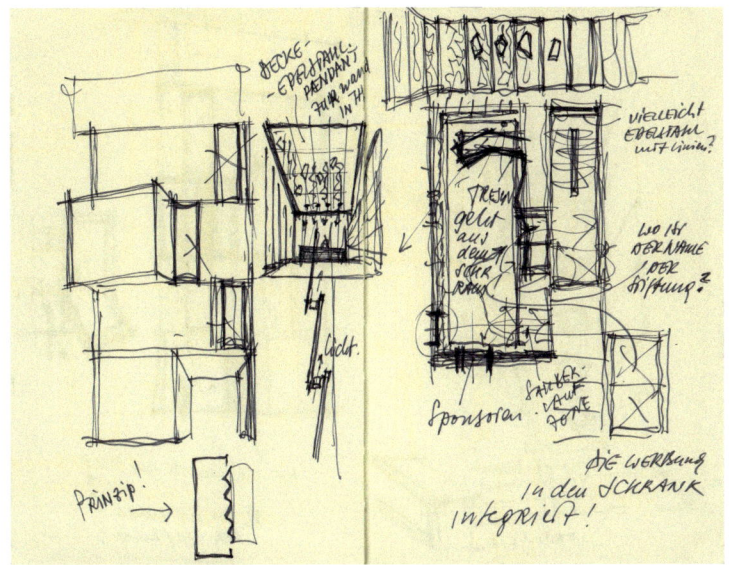

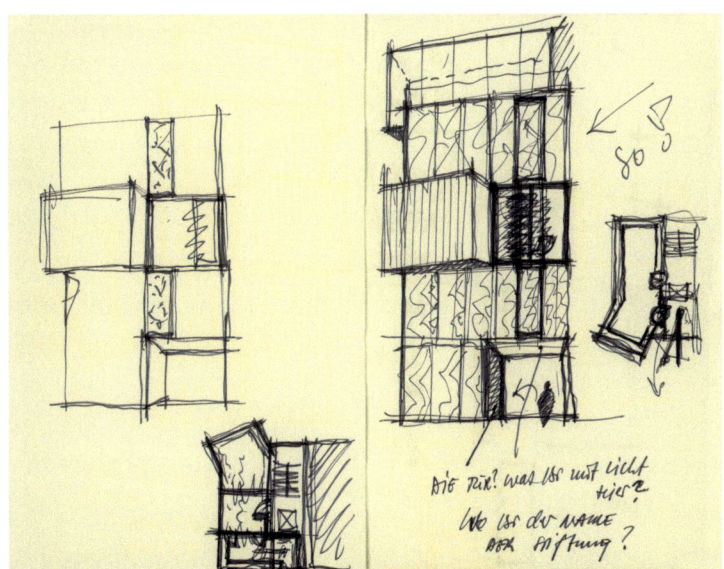

SKETCHES FOR THE MUSEUM FOR ARCHITECTURAL DRAWING,
PAGES FROM A SKETCHBOOK, FELT PEN ON PAPER, 2010,
TCHOBAN FOUNDATION

The design process was somehow different to my previous projects. I'd already spent a long time thinking about it in some depth, so there wasn't a single, initial sketch representing my ideas but a series of four, quite detailed, monochrome drawings, which on the one hand were visions, but on the other clearly expressed the architectural language of the museum. These drawings are now in the museum's collection. In these initial drawings, I had already decided on a geometric structure made up of different cubes adorned with reliefs of architectural drawings. All of this was expressed in them, and one of them even depicts the exact corner position. These drawings also answered the question regarding the role of the museum in a historical context. With its modern architectural language, the building enters into a dialogue with the robust, highly detailed, historical building stock from the 19th century. As I said, it's about the harmony of contrasts.

Then there was the process of realisation.

Using the original drawings, we – as is usual – submitted a preliminary planning application, which was approved by the local building authorities. There were initially problems with some local residents who found the building too closed and wanted it to have more windows. I was finally able to convince them that a museum needs more hanging space than windows, not to mention the excessive light that more windows would entail, which would damage the drawings.

Was a plot of less than a hundred square metres not too small for a museum with an exhibition area, archive and office space?

It was the perfect convergence between what the foundation could afford and the intended exhibition concept, which was devised for such a size. For me, there was absolutely no reason to try and find a larger site. To be honest, it couldn't have been more ideal: a plot facing the street, making the museum very visible. But quite quickly I noticed that my requirements kept growing with my decision to realise the Museum for Architectural Drawing on this site.

How should the building appear in order to express its purpose through its design?

After all, visibility is a major aspect in raising the awareness of the institution and generating interest in the subject of architectural drawing.

What were the reasons behind your decision to choose irregularly stacked cubes as the design for the museum?

When I was considering the design, I started with the idea of the drawing cabinet. That was the core of my design, and the entire building is pieced together like this. These drawing cabinets form a unit from which the form of the building evolves. It was very important to me that you could read the façade of each floor and roughly know what was happening behind it. The narrow façade openings on the ground floor allude to the façade of the small entrance hall. Then there are the two windowless exhibition floors. Each floor is cantilevered in a different place, making it appear like an independent element of a building whose floor plan is specified by the projection of the cantilevers, giving it an engaging, playful appearance. Above, on the fourth floor, is the archive, also designed as a drawing cabinet – and also with a cantilever. The building is completed by a glass cube, which serves as a space for organisational and curatorial work, press conferences and small meetings. The terraces in front of this, which offer a fantastic view of the Pfefferberg area and beyond, are formed by the two-sided recess of the staggered storey.

TCHOBAN FOUNDATION. MUSEUM FOR ARCHITECTURAL DRAWING, BERLIN, 2013

MUSEUM FOR ARCHITECTURAL DRAWING

DETAIL FAÇADE

DETAIL FAÇADE

The Museum for Architectural Drawing

The stacked cube is a recurring architectural motif as seen, for example, in the New Museum of Contemporary Art in New York, designed by the Japanese architecture firm SANAA.

That's true, but I don't think there are any genuinely new forms in architecture. It's about interpretation, it's about detail, it's about how you actually read the motif or even the tradition. Most architecture uses the right angle at some point. There are a lot of buildings that use the same architectural language, but their visual appearance and the distinctiveness of their creative expression – right down to the smallest detail – always lead to the creation of something unique. I think that this also applies to the Museum for Architectural Drawing.

Let's talk about the structure and composition of the façade.

That's a particularly important aspect for me, one we have already discussed in general in our second conversation. Unlike non-bearing, so-called "rear-ventilated" façades, which can be found on many conventional buildings, the façade of the Museum for Architectural Drawing doesn't just operate as a skin but is actually the load-bearing structure of the building. I find it a real shame when the façade only has a cladding function and isn't load-bearing. You can always see this if you have a trained eye. With the Museum for Architectural Drawing, the concrete cubes are actually the load-bearing base of the building. This isn't just important to me personally, it is also an essential contribution when it comes to sustainable measures in construction. Sadly, this technique is not used very often in new builds.

"For me, this project has always been about dialogue, the interplay between interior and exterior."

The concrete reliefs are the main stylistic device of the façade. The Russian architectural historian Grigory Revzin talks vividly about an "aesthetic which is entirely unexpected for architecture – the aesthetic of the graphic line, the movement of the line, the pressure of the pen or pencil". All of these reliefs show sections of drawings from your collection. Which artists and works did you choose to feature on the façade?

The idea with the reliefs came quite spontaneously. When I was doing my first sketches for the building, the cubes suddenly seemed so lifeless, which led to the idea of decorating the concrete structures with reliefs. The motifs I chose were details of drawings that I acquired early on in my collection. There is a set design by Pietro di Gottardo Gonzaga [1751–1831], an artist and stage designer who was particularly important to me during my studies in Saint Petersburg. As I mentioned earlier, I was fascinated by his way of drawing, a special ink-painting technique. I'm extremely happy that we were able to successfully bring this technique across in the reliefs on the façade.

We spoke in detail about Pietro Gonzaga in our third conversation – he was a role model for your creative work. Which other artist has gained pride of place on the façade of the museum?

The other artist, Angelo Toselli [c. 1765–1827] from Bologna, who later went on to achieve fame in Russia, was also a set designer and a contemporary of Gonzaga. In total, there are three drawings by these two artists that I chose to feature in the façade reliefs, with different details spreading across the different floors. It was important for me to choose sections of the drawings that have a perspectival effect, since this gives the façade a further, artificial, depth, so to speak.

ANGELO TOSELLI, STAGE DESIGN WITH THE INTERIOR OF THE GOTHIC HALL FOR THE BOLSHOI THEATRE IN SAINT PETERSBURG, PEN, BROWN WASH AND INK, 1818, SERGEI TCHOBAN COLLECTION

The Museum for Architectural Drawing

When you were designing the museum, you also wanted the dialogue between inside and outside to be readable across all floors. You realised this using many different creative techniques.

For me, this project has always been about dialogue, the interplay between interior and exterior. In keeping with this idea, motifs on the concrete façade can also be found in the entrance hall, for example, but engraved in walnut. I tried to make this harmony of contrasts perceptible on many layers. There is the cold, heavy concrete façade on the outside, the light, delicate drawings on the inside, and a contrast-rich transition between these two worlds with the foyer, as a harmonious whole, acting as a channel between the two worlds.

Entering the foyer of the museum, with its inlays of polished, dark walnut on the one side and the elongated, glazed bookcases made from the same wood on the other, one is overcome by a sensation of warmth and comfort. It reminds me of your description of the library rooms in the Russian Academy of Arts in Saint Petersburg. Did this formative experience inspire your design for the interior of this space?

Yes, it did. When I first visited the library of the Academy of Arts during my student days, it was an overwhelming and unforgettable moment. I can still remember the stark contrast between the long, relatively light and noticeably colder library corridor and the darker rooms within, which radiate a particular warmth and somehow seem to embrace the visitor. I also tried to recreate this special experience through the design of the foyer of my museum and generate a similar, emotionally encompassing atmosphere for the visitor.

The Museum for Architectural Drawing

ENTRANCE OF THE MUSEUM FOR ARCHITECTURAL DRAWING

FOYER OF THE MUSEUM FOR ARCHITECTURAL DRAWING

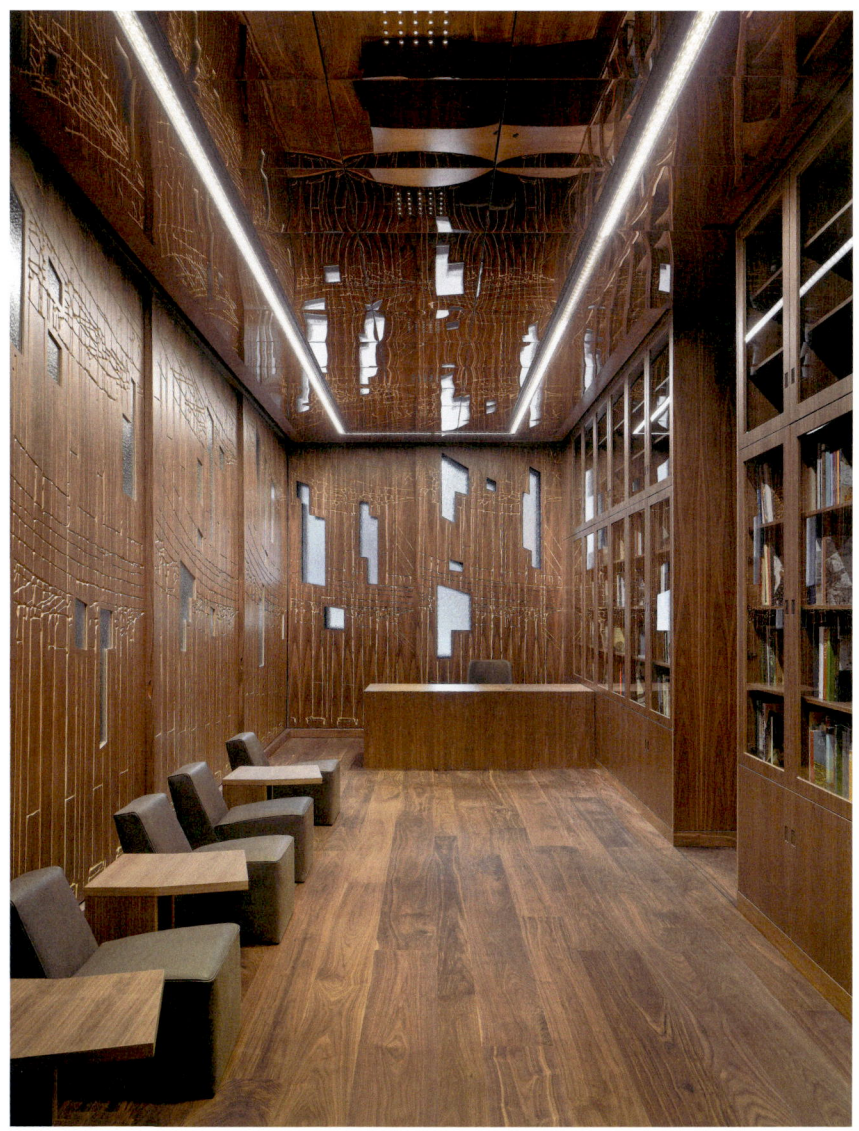

FOYER

The Museum for Architectural Drawing

PETER COOK AT THE OPENING OF THE EXHIBITION "PETER COOK. RETROSPECTIVE", BERLIN, 2016

ÁLVARO SIZA AT THE OPENING OF THE EXHIBITION "SIZA – UNSEEN & UNKNOWN", BERLIN, 2019

Can you describe to the reader how the museum's exhibition programme is decided upon?

The Museum for Architectural Drawing is a charitable organisation with a board of trustees – comprising the art historian Eva-Maria Barkhofen, you and myself – that decides on the exhibition programme and other relevant questions concerning the museum. This is the best basis for an intensive and constructive collaboration. Proposals come from the members of the board as well as from external curators and other interested institutions. An important aspect of this process is alternating exhibitions of contemporary artists with those of historical positions. Now and again there are exhibitions that expand the scope of pure architectural drawing, for example *Anime Architecture*, which was about drawings for Japanese animated films, or the exhibition on German film architecture in the Weimar Republic.

Which aspect of the museum work is most important to you?

Something that plays a major role for me is the fact that today's museums aren't just about preserving and exhibiting, but also about education. This means putting on events to accompany the exhibitions, like podium discussions with art and architectural historians, or workshops and guided tours that place the exhibitions in a wider cultural, historical and socio-political context. That is why joint events with Aedes are also a fantastic addition. Exhibition openings at our museum are often accompanied by podium discussions at the Aedes Network Campus, expanding the themes of the exhibitions, for example with Peter Cook, Álvaro Siza or Lebbeus Woods.

The Museum for Architectural Drawing

Today, both our exhibition venues – the Tchoban Foundation for outstanding architectural drawing and the Aedes Architecture Forum for contemporary architectural and urban concepts – are well-known cultural institutions that complement each other and collaborate with each other in many ways.

In recent years the Museum for Architectural Drawing has also expanded its work with children, young people and students – with an increasing amount of success.

It's especially important to us to introduce children and young people to the subject of architectural drawing in an exciting and playful way and actively include them in our workshops. The children often take home their own drawings with a huge sense of pride. But this also means that with every exhibition you have to adapt the contents of the programme using new ideas and concepts tailored to children and young people.

Are there also student groups among the visitors?

Since they are generally art and architecture students, they also tend to just visit the museum without any specially tailored programmes or participating in thematic guided tours. For them, there is the fascination of experiencing original drawings of great masters – that many are familiar with from books – for the first time. In this way, the museum also becomes a place of teaching. I am especially pleased about the increasing number of architecture students visiting the museum, because they can experience the creative process of drawing with their own eyes and maybe incorporate it into their own working practice. Whilst drawing is not the only way to achieve good architecture, it is definitely one way, and students are able to learn that here and hopefully at university too.

EDUCATIONAL PROGRAMME OF THE TCHOBAN FOUNDATION FOR CHILDREN

"For me personally, the reactions of the exhibition visitors are especially important."

Do you have an overview of general visitor interest?

After each exhibition we look at visitor numbers, comments in the guestbook, media coverage and feedback on social networks. I'm extremely happy about the growing number of visitors, even though I know that the success of a museum isn't measured by this alone. For me personally, the reactions of the exhibition visitors are especially important. I often walk through the museum as a visitor, so to speak; not to look at the exhibits – I know them well enough already – but to see the intensity and curiosity with which people immerse themselves in the drawings.

In a short time, your museum has become an accepted exhibition partner of many outstanding, internationally renowned museums such as the Victoria and Albert Museum in London, Le Cabinet des Dessins Jean Bonna at the École Nationale Supérieure des Beaux-Arts de Paris, the Albertina in Vienna, the German Architecture Museum (DAM) in Frankfurt am Main, the Architectural Museum of the Technische Universität Berlin and the Sir John Soane's Museum in London. That's a remarkable development.

We had already been in contact with some of these museums for quite a while, since we had shown exhibitions there before we founded our museum. This enabled the gradual forging of many trusting relationships, like, as you mentioned, with the Sir John Soane's Museum in London, which eventually led to us being able to open the Museum for Architectural Drawing with the exhibition *Piranesi's Paestum – Master Drawings Uncovered*, featuring rarely shown original drawings by Giovanni Battista Piranesi. Of course, the infrastructure of the museum is also an important factor in such collaborations.

The Museum for Architectural Drawing

PIRANESI'S PAESTUM – MASTER DRAWINGS UNCOVERED. EXHIBITION OF THE SIR JOHN SOANE'S MUSEUM, LONDON, TCHOBAN FOUNDATION. MUSEUM FOR ARCHITECTURAL DRAWING, BERLIN, 2013

In a broader sense, the spatial provision of the museum is also part of the museum's concept. Has that been confirmed through your experience of the different in-house and guest exhibitions so far?

Yes, totally. Our museum is small but equipped with very modern facilities in terms of conservation and climatic conditions, the lighting in the exhibition spaces and the security system. But we also have another advantage: because the logistics, preparation times and set-ups at our museum take up far less time and effort in comparison to larger institutions, it means we can implement things more quickly. We can show relatively small exhibitions with up to 40 drawings and that will fill the museum – a treasure trove, so to speak. As I said, the amount of organisation is quite manageable. It also means that our museum has opened up a new field that didn't exist before. With the Piranesi exhibition, for instance, we exhibited 15 works on two floors. But it was in no way too few, because each of these drawings had a kind of "Mona Lisa" effect, and the darkened rooms created an intimate proximity between viewer and image. I believe that all these aspects contribute to the fact that museums like the Albertina in Vienna and the German Architecture Museum in Frankfurt like to work with us and exhibit at our museum.

In the years since the museum opened, have you thought about showing your own creative work – which is exhibited in major museums across the world – here, in your own museum?

Never! That would be totally counter-productive, absurd even. I didn't set up the Museum for Architectural Drawing to promote myself, I did it to provide a platform for the art of architectural drawing. It's important to me that the museum's directors and curators value my creative work but make a completely independent decision as to whether to exhibit it – or not. Even as the founder of such an institute and being in part responsible for the exhibition programme, independence is paramount. Another approach would be unimaginable. This is the only way to create a diverse exhibition programme and introduce the visitor to new, unknown worlds using the magic of architectural drawing.

You have established the non-profit Tchoban Foundation, designed and built the Museum for Architectural Drawing, developed a world-renowned exhibition programme with your board of trustees, continually expanded your collection, your work is exhibited in major museums around the world, and now you are set to take on a new challenge: at the end of 2018 you were appointed onto the board of directors at the American Society of Architectural Illustrators, ASAI, and from 2020 you will assume the presidency there. This also means that the "Architecture in Perspective" conference will take place in Berlin in autumn 2020, and an exhibition of its selected works will be shown in your museum. Voting you in as the president of this institution is a significant step in the evolution of the ASAI: its opening towards Europe. What do you see as your central tasks in this important position?

Firstly, this appointment is a great honour, as I have been actively involved in the work and competitions of the ASAI throughout the past 26 years. I consider the ASAI to be a vital institution in preserving the culture of architectural drawing. Lebbeus Woods, Steve Oles, Thomas Schaller, Gilbert Gorski, Syd Mead and many other notable American artists were and are part of the ASAI network. With this move towards Berlin, I see it as my responsibility – and it will be a great pleasure for me – to contribute to the American Society of Architectural Illustrators becoming known and recognised as a major international institution in the promotion of architectural drawing in Europe.

PIRANESI'S PAESTUM – MASTER DRAWINGS UNCOVERED

The Museum for Architectural Drawing

"To dedicate my life
to architecture in all its facets,
as architect, draughtsman,
collector and founder of the
Museum for Architectural Drawing
is an invaluable gift. It is a profound
pleasure for me to share the
fascination for the art of architectural
drawings with all those who are
visiting the museum or reading this
publication. With both, I also hope
to inspire as many people as possible
to awaken in them an awareness
for architecture and its primary
goal: to improve the everyday living
conditions for everyone."

The Museum for Architectural Drawing

TCHOBAN FOUNDATION. MUSEUM FOR ARCHITECTURAL DRAWING, BERLIN, 2013

TCHOBAN FOUNDATION. MUSEUM FOR ARCHITECTURAL DRAWING, BERLIN, 2013

Appendix

Vita

Kristin Feireiss (Dr. h.c.)
Curator, editor and author

Born in 1942 in Berlin. She studied Art History and Philosophy.
Feireiss is an architecture curator, author and publisher as well as the founder (together with Helga Retzer, † 1984) and director (together with Hans-Jürgen Commerell) of the first independent architecture gallery in the world, Aedes Architecture Forum in Berlin.

1996–2001	Director of the Netherlands Architecture Institute in Rotterdam (in addition to Aedes)
1996 & 2000	Commissioner of the Dutch Pavilion at the Venice Biennale of Architecture
2013–2017	Jury member of the Pritzker Architecture Prize
Since 2018	Member of the Advisory Board of Berlin International University of Applied Science
Since 2018	Member of the Board of Trustees of the Stiftung Exilmuseum Berlin
2019	Jury member of the Russian Biennale of Young Architects, Kazan

Distinctions

2001	Cross of the Order of Merit of the Federal Republic of Germany
2007	Honorary Doctorate of the Technische Universität Carolo-Wilhelmina, Braunschweig
2013	Knight in the Order of the Netherlands Lion
2016	Austrian Decoration of Honor for Science and Art
2016	Honorary Member of the Royal Institute of British Architects, RIBA, London
2017	Honorary Member of the Architecture Association of Germany, BDA, Berlin

Aedes contributes with exhibitions and publications to an extended understanding of architecture and urban design, including their cultural, social and economic factors.

As director of the Netherlands Architecture Institute (NAi) Feireiss brought greater attention to urban transformation processes and carried out groundbreaking research in this area, especially in Japan and South Africa, accompanied by exhibitions, publications and symposia.

Her most important concern, however, is to awaken interest in the broader public for architecture and urban design and to raise awareness of the fact that the built environment concerns everyone.

In 2009 Kristin Feireiss, together with her partner Hans-Jürgen Commerell, initiated the Aedes Network Campus Berlin (ANCB), an urban laboratory where universities from all over the world come together for workshops and where questions of current urban and societal developments are discussed in various public formats such as conferences, symposia and lectures.

Selected Publications

Feireiss, who was a member of the European Cultural Parliament for several years, has edited numerous monographs and thematic volumes on architecture and the urban context:

Informal City: Caracas Case, which sheds light on the potential of informal housing.

Architecture in Times of Need, which highlights the reconstruction and revitalisation of New Orleans, Lower Ninth Ward after Hurricane Katrina.

She also co-edited the publication *Architecture of Change: Sustainability and Humanity in the Built Environment.*

KRISTIN FEIREISS

Vita
Deyan Sudjic
Architect, curator, architecture critic, author and editor

Deyan Sudjic was born in 1952 in London and earned his Diploma in Architecture from Edinburgh University.

1981	Architecture critic for the *Sunday Times*
1983–1986	Founding Editor of *Blueprint* magazine
1992	Visiting Professor at the University of Applied Arts in Vienna
1992–1998	Architecture critic for *The Guardian*
1996–2000	Director of Glasgow 1999 UK City of Architecture and Design
2000–2004	Editor of *Domus*
2000–2006	Architecture critic for *The Observer*
2002	Director of the Venice Biennale of Architecture
2005–2010	Visiting Professor at the Royal College of Art
2005–2006	Dean of the Faculty of Art, Design and Architecture, Kingston University
Since 2009	Professor of Design and Architectural Studies at Lancaster University
Since 2017	Honorary Trustee at the Norman Foster Foundation

He is Honorary Fellow of the Royal Institute of British Architects and Honorary Fellow, Royal Incorporation of Architects in Scotland.

Exhibitions

Deyan Sudjic's portfolio of exhibitions includes, among many others, *Identity and Design* at the Louisiana Museum of Modern Art, Copenhagen; *Design and Democracy* at McLaren Galleries, Glasgow, and at the Design Museum, London:

2007	*Zaha Hadid*
2009	*David Chipperfield Architects: Form Matters*
2019	*Stanley Kubrick: The Exhibition*
2020	*Prada Front and Back*

His career has helped to shape the culture of the modern museum.

For Sudjic, design had to become a more responsive process. His stewardship has steered the museum programme towards more inclusive design and wider audience participation. He is pushing the importance of design as an ambition as well as a social and political expression.

Architecture, urbanism and design have all been his lifelong passions.

Selected Publications

- **2016** *The Language of Cities*, Penguin
- **2014** *B is for Bauhaus*, Penguin
- **2011** *The Endless City*, Phaidon Press, edited with Professor Ricky Burdett
- **1992** *The 100 Mile City*, Harcourt Publishers

DEYAN SUDJIC

Vita
Sergei Tchoban
Architect, artist, collector, museum founder

Born in 1962 in Leningrad (now Saint Petersburg), Russia. He studied Architecture at and graduated from the Repin Institute of Painting, Sculpture, and Architecture of the Russian Academy of Arts in Saint Petersburg. From 1986 onwards he worked as an architect in Russia.

1992–1995	Architect at NPS Nietz – Prasch – Sigl Architekten BDA, Hamburg, Germany
Since 1992	Member of the American Society of Architectural Illustrators (ASAI)
Since 1995	Partner at Nietz – Prasch – Sigl und Partner Architekten BDA, Hamburg, Berlin, Dresden, Germany
Since 1996	Head of the Berlin office within the partnership
Since 2003	Partner at nps tchoban voss Architekten BDA, Hamburg, Berlin, Dresden, Germany
2006	Head of architecture firm SPEECH, Moscow, Russia
2009	Founder of the Tchoban Foundation – Museum for Architectural Drawing, Berlin, Germany
Since 2014	Honorary member of the Russian Academy of Arts, St Petersburg, Russia
2017	Founder of the Russian Architecture Biennial for Young Architects, Kazan, Russia
Since 2017	Partner at TCHOBAN VOSS Architekten GmbH, Hamburg, Berlin, Dresden, Germany
2020	President of the American Society of Architectural Illustrators (ASAI)

SERGEI TCHOBAN

Group Exhibitions
Architecture

2020   The annual exhibition da! Architecture in and from Berlin 2020
curator: Chamber of Architects Berlin;
stilwerk, Berlin, Germany

2018   The annual exhibition da! Architecture in and from Berlin 2018
curator: Chamber of Architects Berlin;
stilwerk, Berlin, Germany

2017   The annual exhibition da! Architecture in and from Berlin 2017
curator: Chamber of Architects Berlin;
stilwerk, Berlin, Germany

2016   The annual exhibition da! Architecture in and from Berlin 2016
curator: Chamber of Architects Berlin;
stilwerk, Berlin, Germany

2015   Architecture of Saint Petersburg 2015
organiser: Saint Petersburg Union of Architects of Russia;
Russian Museum of Ethnography, Saint Petersburg, Russia

2014   This is modern
curators: Matthias Schirren, Paul Kahlfeldt, Claudia Kromrei;
exhibition of Deutscher Werkbund;
14th Venice Biennale of Architecture, Palazzo Ca'Tron, Venice, Italy

2013   Architecture of Saint Petersburg 2013
organiser: Saint Petersburg Union of Architects of Russia;
Russian Museum of Ethnography, Saint Petersburg, Russia

2012   i-city / i-land
curator: Sergei Tchoban, co-curators: Valeria Kashirina, Sergey Kuznetsov;
commissar: Grigory Revzin;
Russian Pavilion, 13th Venice Biennale of Architecture;
Giardini della Biennale, Venice, Italy

2011   Architecture of Saint Petersburg 2011
organiser: Saint Petersburg Union of Architects of Russia;
Russian Museum of Ethnography, Saint Petersburg, Russia

Evgeny Gerasimov and Partners XX
curators: Valeria Kashirina, Darija Lozmanova;
Russian Museum of Ethnography, Saint Petersburg, Russia

The annual exhibition da! Architecture in and from Berlin 2011
curator: Chamber of Architects Berlin;
stilwerk, Berlin, Germany

2010   **Factory Russia**
curators: Sergei Tchoban, Pavel Khoroshilov, Grigory Revzin;
in collaboration with Sergey Kuznetsov, Valeria Kashirina;
Russian Pavilion, 12th Venice Biennale of Architecture;
Giardini della Biennale, Venice, Italy

Modernising the Panel Building. Experience from Germany
curators: Christine Gräwe, Valeria Kashirina;
ARCH Moscow 2010, 2nd Moscow Architecture Biennale;
Central House of the Artist, Moscow, Russia

2009   **Architecture of Saint Petersburg 2009**
organiser: Saint Petersburg Union of Architects of Russia;
Russian Museum of Ethnography, Saint Petersburg, Russia

Emergency Reserve. Industrial Architecture of the Past: a Resource for the Future
curator: Irina Shipova;
17th International Architecture Festival Zodchestvo 2009;
Manezh Central Exhibition Hall, Moscow, Russia

European Embankment. The New Dance Theatre Precinct in Saint Petersburg
curators: Valeria Kashirina, Andreas Oehme;
Architekturforum Aedes Pfefferberg, Berlin, Germany

RodDom
(BornHouse)
curator: Yuri Avvakumov;
Église Sainte Marie-Madeleine, Lille, France

The Rediscovery of Sretenka. A Moscow Urban District in a State of Change
curator: Sergei Tchoban;
Aedes Land, Berlin, Germany

2008   **ARChess**
(Chess-Play for Russia)
curators: Pavel Khoroshilov, Grigory Revzin;
11th Venice Biennale of Architecture, Giardini della Biennale, Venice, Italy

RodDom
(BornHouse)
curator: Yuri Avvakumov;
Chiesa di San Stae, Venice, Italy

The annual exhibition da! Architecture in and from Berlin 2008
curator: Chamber of Architects Berlin;
stilwerk, Berlin, Germany

2007   **Architecture of Saint Petersburg 2007**
organiser: Saint Petersburg Union of Architects of Russia;
Russian Museum of Ethnography, Saint Petersburg, Russia

RodDom
(BornHouse)
curator: Yuri Avvakumov;
Vkhutemas Gallery, Moscow, Russia

RodDom
(BornHouse)
curator: Yuri Avvakumov;
Peter and Paul Fortress, Saint Petersburg, Russia

2006 **High Society – Aktuelle Hochhausarchitektur und der Internationale Hochhaus Preis 2006**
(High Society: Current Highrise Architecture and the International Highrise Award 2006)
curator: Deutsches Architekturmuseum (DAM), in cooperation with Peter Schweger;
Deutsches Architekturmuseum (DAM), Frankfurt am Main, Germany

The annual exhibition da! Architecture in and from Berlin 2006
curator: Chamber of Architects Berlin;
stilwerk, Berlin, Germany

2005 **PlayGround**
curator: Yuri Avvakumov;
Design Centre ARTPLAY, Moscow, Russia

2004 **Berlin im Fluss – Architektur und Städtebau entlang der Spree**
(Berlin floating: architecture and urban development along the river Spree)
curator: Philipp Meuser;
Shchusev Museum of Architecture, Moscow, Russia

The annual exhibition da! Architecture in and from Berlin 2004
curator: Chamber of Architects Berlin;
stilwerk, Berlin, Germany

2003 **50 Projects from New Berlin**
curator: Philipp Meuser;
Shchusev Museum of Architecture, Moscow, Russia

Best Moscow Architects, Interarch 2003
curator: International Academy of Architecture (IAA);
Interarch 2003, exhibition of the International Academy of Architecture Moscow (MAAM);
10th World Triennial of Architecture, Sofia, Bulgaria

Idea, Process, Space
curators: Berlin Architecture Union (B.A.U.);
ARCH Moscow 2003, contribution by the Berlin Architecture Union (B.A.U.) and Architekturforum Aedes Berlin, together with Kuehn Bauer Partner, Assmann Salomon, Kiefer, Leonhardt, Andrä und Partner, Meuser Architekten;
Central House of the Artist, Moscow, Russia

The annual exhibition da! Architecture in and from Berlin 2003
curator: Chamber of Architects Berlin;
Passerelle Potsdamer Platz, Berlin, Germany

2002 The annual exhibition da! Architecture in and from Berlin 2002
curator: Chamber of Architects Berlin;
Passerelle Potsdamer Platz, Berlin, Germany

Group Exhibitions
Drawings, installations / art objects

2019 AVANTI-AVANTI-100: Bewegung als Traum
(AVANTI-AVANTI-100: movement as dream)
curator: Dr Wita Noack;
Mies van der Rohe House, Berlin, Germany

BRICS Brasil 2019 Exhibition, 11th BRICS Summit
curator: Luiz Ernesto Meyer Pereira;
Ministry of Foreign Affairs Brazil, Itamaraty Palace, Brasilia, Brazil

The Drawn City
curator: Ekaterina Shalina;
Zaryadie Park Exhibition Hall, Moscow, Russia

2018 Imprint of the Future: Sergei Tchoban and Ioann Zelenin
curator: Mariya Elkina;
part of the Saint Petersburg 2103 exhibition project;
Manezh Central Exhibition Hall, St Petersburg, Russia

The Architecture Drawing Prize 2018
curators: Make Architects, Sir John Soane's House, World Architecture Festival;
Sir John Soane's Museum, London, UK

The Drawing Show
curator: Dr Dora Epstein-Jones;
Yale School of Architecture, New Haven, Connecticut, USA

2017 City DNA
authors: Sergei Tchoban, Sergey Kuznetsov;
in collaboration with Agniya Sterligova;
exhibition by INTERNI;
Università degli Studi Milano, Milan, Italy

2016 Himmel über Berlin. 40/40
(Heaven over Berlin. 40/40)
curators: Andrew Alberts, Armin Behles, Urs Füssler, Heike Hanada;
BDA Galerie, Berlin

Solo Italia. Architettura e paesaggio culturale. Disegni dal Settecento ad Oggi
(Only Italy! Architectural graphics of the 18th–21st centuries)
curators: Rita Bernini, Nina Markova, Galina Tzedrik;
exhibition by the Tchoban Foundation, the Istituto Centrale per la Grafica di Roma, and the Tretyakov Gallery;
Museo dell' Istituto Centrale per la Grafica, Rome, Italy

The Drawing Show
curators: Dr Dora Epstein-Jones;
A+D Architecture and Design Museum, Los Angeles, California, USA

Towers
authors: Sergei Tchoban, Sergey Kuznetsov;
in collaboration with Agniya Sterligova;
exhibition by INTERNI;
Università degli Studi Milano, Milan, Italy

2015 **Living Line**
authors: Sergei Tchoban, Sergey Kuznetsov;
in collaboration with Agniya Sterligova;
exhibition by INTERNI;
Università degli Studi Milano, Milan, Italy

Treasure, Legacy: A Museum for Architectural Drawing
curator: Prof Mark Morris;
Cornell University College of Architecture, Art and Planning, Ithaca, New York, USA

2014 **All about Italy! / Only Italy! Architectural Graphics of the 18th–21st centuries**
curators: Nina Markova, Irina Sedova;
Tretyakov Gallery, Moscow, Russia

U-Cloud
authors: Sergei Tchoban, Sergey Kuznetsov;
in collaboration with Agniya Sterligova;
exhibition by INTERNI;
Università degli Studi Milano, Milan, Italy

2014–2019 **Ken Roberts Memorial Delineation Competition (KRob)**
awards exhibitions 2019, 2017, 2016, 2014
Dallas, Texas, USA

2013 **Golden River**
authors: Sergei Tchoban, Sergey Kuznetsov;
in collaboration with Agniya Sterligova;
exhibition by INTERNI;
Università degli Studi Milano, Milan, Italy

Northern Vision. Master Drawings from the Tchoban Foundation
curators: Nadejda Bartels, Dr Jerzy J. Kierkúc-Bieliński;
Sir John Soane's Museum, London, UK

2012	**12 Architects Design Furniture** Orgatec 2012, Cologne Fair, Cologne, Germany
	Library of Architecture curator: Dmitry Yurievich Ozerkov; The Hermitage, St Petersburg, Russia
	The Architect's Eye authors: Sergei Tchoban, Sergey Kuznetsov; exhibition by INTERNI; Università degli Studi Milano, Milan, Italy
	The Architect's Eye authors: Sergei Tchoban, Sergey Kuznetsov; ARCH Moscow 2012; Central House of the Artist, Moscow, Russia
2011	**Duravit Design Days 2011** Duravit Design Centre, Hornberg, Germany
	Reliquarium curator: Yurij Avvakumov; Design Centre ARTPLAY, Moscow, Russia
2008	**The Aura of Design** curators: Vladimir Frolov, Valeria Kashirina; Aura Design Centre, St Petersburg, Russia
1999	**Fünf gezeichnete Welten – Five Drawn Worlds** **Gorski / Gothe / van den Hoed / Schaller / Tchoban** curator: Sergei Tchoban; Galerie Aedes East, Berlin, Germany
1995	**Architecture in Perspective 09. Drawing the Future** exhibition of the American Society of Architectural Illustrators (ASAI); Galerie Aedes West, Berlin, Germany
1992–2019	**Architecture in Perspective** annual exhibitions of the American Society of Architectural Illustrators (ASAI), No. 34/2019, No. 33/2018, No. 32/2017, No. 31/2016, No. 30/2015, No. 29/2014, No. 28/2013, No. 27/2012, No. 25/2010, No. 23/2008, No. 22/2007, No. 21/2006, No. 19/2004, No. 16/2001, No. 15/2000, No. 14/1999, No. 13/1998, No. 10/1995, No. 09/1994, No. 08/1993 and No. 07/1992); USA and Canada
1990	**Architekturdarstellung und Architekturvisionen** (Architectural representation and architectural visions) curators: BDA Hamburg; Hamburg University of Applied Sciences, Hamburg, Germany

Solo Exhibitions
Architecture

2020 **Une ville dessineé**
(A drawn city)
curator: Valeria Kashirina, co-curator: Esenija Bannan;
La Galerie d' Architecture, Paris, France

2017 **Tchoban Voss Architekten. Bilder aus Berlin**
(Tchoban Voss Architekten. Pictures from Berlin)
curator: Valeria Kashirina;
Architektur Galerie Berlin, Berlin, Germany

2016 **SPEECH Project**
curators: SPEECH;
Multimedia Art Museum, Moscow, Russia

2015 **Realtà e Fantasia: Cartoline dall'Italia**
(Reality and fantasy: postcards from Italy)
curators: Alessandro Benetti, Valeria Kashirina, Luca Molinari;
SpazioFMG per l'Architettura, Milan, Italy

2013 **ARCH Moscow 2013 – Architect of the Year**
Central House of the Artist, Moscow, Russia

2009 **nps tchoban voss – Internationale Projekte**
(nps tchoban voss: international projects)
curators: Axel Neubauer, Andreas Oehme;
Hamburg Architecture Summer 2009;
Fachbuchhandlung Sautter + Lackmann, Hamburg, Germany

2008 **Architekturachse Russland–Deutschland**
(Architectural axes Russia/Germany)
curator: Valeria Kashirina;
Deutsche Woche 2008, Union of Architects, Saint Petersburg, Russia

Berlin – Moscow
curator: Valeria Kashirina;
Sochi Art Museum, Sochi, Russian

Sergei Tchoban - zeichnen planen bauen
(Sergei Tchoban: draw, plan, build)
curator: Valeria Kashirina;
Deutsche Werkstätten Hellerau, Dresden, Germany

2007 **Architecture for the City / Peter Schweger and Sergei Tchoban**
curators: Valeria Kashirina, Bernhard Kroll;
Museum of the Academy of Arts, Saint Petersburg, Russia

2006 **Federation Tower. Peter Schweger und Sergei Tchoban**
(Federation Tower. Peter Schweger and Sergei Tchoban)
curators: Valeria Kashirina, Bernhard Kroll;
Deutsches Architektur Zentrum (DAZ), Berlin, Germany

2005 **Berlin – Moskau / Москва – Берлин**
(Berlin – Moscow / Moscow – Berlin)
curator: Valeria Kashirina;
Galerie Aedes East, Berlin, Germany

Peter Schweger. Sergei Tchoban. Federation Tower;
curators: Valeria Kushlrina, Bernhard Kroll;
Shchusev Museum of Architecture, Moscow, Russian

1997 **Der Java Turm**
(The Java Tower)
Galerie Aedes East, Berlin, Germany

Solo Exhibitions
Drawing

2019 **Draw Art Fair London 2019**
curator: Jill Silverman;
Saatchi Gallery, London, UK

Open Borders. Bienal Internacional de Arte Contemporânea de Curitiba 2019
curator: Tereza de Arruda, co-curator: Esenija Bannan;
Oscar Niemeyer Museum, Curitiba, Brazil

Sergei Tchoban: Drawing Buildings/Building Drawings
curators: Vladimir Belogolovsky, Valeria Kashirina;
Tsinghua University, Beijing, China

2018 **Capricci Russi: Drawings by Sergei Tchoban and the tradition of the architectural fantasy**
curator: Jan-Philipp Frühsorge;
La Biennale del Disegno di Rimini, Fabbrica Arte Rimini (FAR), Rimini, Italy

Den-City – Urban Landscape
curator: Matteo Vercelloni;
Galleria Antonia Jannone Disegni di Architettura, Milan, Italy

Dreams of Frozen Music – The Architectural Drawings of Sergei Tchoban
curator: Jan-Philipp Frühsorge;
Tokyo Art Museum, Tokyo, Japan

Sergei Tchoban: Contrasting Harmony of the City
curators: Esenija Bannan, Jolanta Gromadzka;
Museum of Architecture, Wrocław, Poland

Sergei Tchoban: Drawing Buildings/Building Drawings
curators: Vladimir Belogolovsky;
Gallery of Shanghai Study Center, Shanghai, China

Sergei Tchoban: Visions/Projections
curators: Thomas Geuder, Valeria Kashirina;
Raumgalerie, Stuttgart, Germany

2017 **Puentes y Agujas**
(Bridges and spires)
curator: Vladimir Belogolovsky;
XVI Bienal Internacional de Arquitectura de Buenos Aires;
Galeria la Usina des Arte, Buenos Aires, Argentina

Sergei Tchoban: Architectural Drawings
curators: Dr Dora Epstein-Jones, Esenija Bannan;
A+D Architecture and Design Museum, Los Angeles, California, USA

2016 **Sergei Tchoban: Bridges and Spires – Drawing Reflections on Past and Future**
curator: Vladimir Belogolovsky;
InCITE Gallery, Bangalore, India

2015 **Glazing the Future. Sergei Tchoban's Architectural Fantasies**
curators: Valeria Kashirina, Anna Martovitskaya;
Square – Brussels Convention Centre, Brussels, Belgium

Realtà e Fantasia: Cartoline dall'Italia
(Reality and fantasy: postcards from Italy)
curators: Alessandro Benetti, Valeria Kashirina, Luca Molinari;
SpazioFMG per l'Architettura, Milan, Italy

2010 **Architekturwelten. Sergei Tchoban – Zeichner und Sammler**
(Architectural worlds. Sergei Tchoban: draughtsman and collector)
curator: Eva-Maria Barkhofen;
Deutsches Architekturmuseum (DAM), Frankfurt am Main, Germany

2009 **Aqua**
curator: Valeria Kashirina;
Galleria Antonia Jannone Disegni di Architettura, Milan, Italy

2008 **Sergei Tchoban – Petersburger Hängung**
(Sergei Tchoban: Saint Petersburg hanging)
curator: Valeria Kashirina;
Galerie Berlin Werkraum, Berlin, Germany

Exhibition Design

2019 **Edvard Munch**
in collaboration with Agniya Sterligova;
Tretyakov Gallery, Moscow, Russia

2018 **La Russia e fatta a modo suo**
(Russian pilgrimage)
in collaboration with Agniya Sterligova;
Vatican Pinacoteca, Vatican, Vatican State

2017 **Giorgio de Chirico. Metaphysical Insights**
in collaboration with Agniya Sterligova;
Tretyakov Gallery, Moscow, Russia

Permanent exhibition at the Museum of the New Jerusalem Monastery
in collaboration with Agniya Sterligova;
Museum of the New Jerusalem Monastery, Istra, Russia

2016 **Roma Aeterna. Masterworks of the Vatican Pinacoteca**
in collaboration with Agniya Sterligova;
Tretyakov Gallery, Moscow, Russia

Vasily Kandinsky. Counterpoint: Composition VI – Composition VII
in collaboration with Agniya Sterligova;
Tretyakov Gallery, Moscow, Russia

2015 **Jan Vanriet – Losing Face**
curator: Sergei Tchoban;
in collaboration with Agniya Sterligova;
Jewish Museum and Tolerance Centre, Moscow, Russia

2014 **The Forge of Great Architecture. Soviet Competitions of the 1920s–50s**
curators: Sergei Tchoban, Irina Chepkunova;
in collaboration with Agniya Sterligova;
Shchusev Museum of Architecture, Moscow, Russia

2012 **i-city / i-land**
curator: Sergei Tchoban, co-curators: Valeriya Kashirina, Sergey Kuznetsov;
commissar: Grigory Revzin;
Russian Pavilion, 13th Venice Biennale of Architecture;
Giardini della Biennale, Venice, Italy

2010 **Factory Russia**
curators: Sergei Tchoban, Grigory Revzin, Pavel Khoroshilov;
Russian Pavilion, 12th Venice Biennale of Architecture;
Giardini della Biennale, Venice, Italy

2009 European Embankment. The New Dance Theatre Precinct in Saint Petersburg
curation and design: Sergei Tchoban, Valeria Kashirina, Andreas Oehme;
Architekturforum Aedes Pfefferberg, Berlin, Germany

The Rediscovery of Sretenka. A Moscow Urban District in a State of Change
curator: Sergei Tchoban;
Aedes Land, Berlin, Germany

2004 **Moscow Archaeology**
curator: Sergei Tchoban;
in collaboration with Julia Neumann;
Shchusev Museum of Architecture, Moscow, Russia

**STADTanSICHTEN – Planschrank Moskau /
ВИД(ение) ГОРОДА – Чертежный архив Москвы**
(CITYvision/VIEWS – Moscow Drawing Archive)
curator and designer: Sergei Tchoban;
in collaboration with Valeria Kashirina, Julia Neumann;
ifa-Galerie Berlin, Berlin, Germany

**STADTanSICHTEN – Planschrank Moskau /
ВИД(ение) ГОРОДА – Чертежный архив Москвы**
(CITYvision/VIEWS – Moscow Drawing Archive)
curator and designer: Sergei Tchoban;
in collaboration with Valeria Kashirina, Julia Neumann;
ifa-Galerie Bonn, Bonn, Germany

**STADTanSICHTEN – Planschrank Moskau /
ВИД(ение) ГОРОДА – Чертежный архив Москвы**
(CITYvision/VIEWS – Moscow Drawing Archive)
curator and designer: Sergei Tchoban;
in collaboration with Valeria Kashirina, Julia Neumann;
ifa-Galerie Stuttgart, Stuttgart, Germany

2003 **Idea, Process, Space**
curators: Berlin Architecture Union (B.A.U.);
ARCH Moscow 2003, contribution by the Berlin Architecture Union (B.A.U.) and Architekturforum Aedes, together with Kuehn Bauer Partner, Assmann Salomon, Kiefer, Leonhardt, Andrä und Partner, Meuser Architekten;
Central House of the Artist, Moscow, Russia

2000 **Raum für Kunst**
(Room for art)
ARCH Moscow 2000;
Central House of Artists, Moscow, Russia

1989 **Young Artists of Russia**
Central House of Artists, Moscow, Russia

1988 **Young Artists of Saint Petersburg**
Union of Artists, Saint Petersburg, Russia

Set Design for Opera

2019 **The Medium**
composer: Gian Carlo Menotti; conductor: Aleksey Vereshchagin;
director: Aleksandr Molochnikov; set design: Sergei Tchoban;
in collaboration with Agniya Sterligova;
Bolshoi Theatre, chamber stage, Moscow, Russia

The Telephone
composer: Gian Carlo Menotti; conductor: Aleksey Vereshchagin;
director: Aleksandr Molochnikov; set design: Sergei Tchoban;
in collaboration with Agniya Sterligova;
Bolshoi Theatre, chamber stage, Moscow, Russia

2017 **The Bright Way, 19.17**
director: Aleksandr Molochnikov; stage design: Sergei Tchoban;
in collaboration with Agniya Sterligova;
MAT (Moscow Art Theatre), Moscow, Russia

Set Design for Film

2017 **Myths**
director: Aleksandr Molochnikov;
set design: Sergei Tchoban;
in collaboration with Jana Katrenko

Exhibitions
Tchoban Foundation
Museum for Architectural Drawing

2020 Jean-François Thomas de Thomon: Drawings for Saint Petersburg
from the Collection of the Art Library – Berlin State Museums
curators: Nadejda Bartels, Elke Blauert

Thom Mayne: Sculptural Drawings
curators: Esenija Bannan, Kristin Feireiss

2019 **German Film Architecture. 1918–1933**
curator: Nadejda Bartels

In the Making: Ilya & Emilia Kabakov. From Drawing to Installation
curator: Esenija Bannan

Siza: Unseen & Unknown
curators: António Choupina, Kristin Feireiss

2018 **Hans Poelzig: Projects for Berlin**
from the collection of the Architecture Museum of the
Technical University of Berlin, Germany;
curators: Nadejda Bartels, Dr Hans-Dieter Nägelke

Opening Lines: Sketchbook of Ten Modern Architects
from the Drawing Matter collection, Somerset, UK;
curators: Dr Tina di Carlo, Niall Hobhouse, Dr Olivia Horsfall Turner

Visions of World Architecture.
Illustrations from the Royal Academy Lectures of Sir John Soane
from the collection of the Sir John Soane's Museum, London, UK;
curator: Prof Dr David Watkin

2017 **Berlin Projects. Architectural Drawings 1920–1990**
from the collection of the Deutsches Architekturmuseum (DAM),
Frankfurt am Main, Germany;
curators: Nadejda Bartels, Inge Wolf

Centrifugal Tendencies. Tallinn – Moscow – Novosibirsk
curators: Yuri Avvakumov, Andres Kurg

Drawing Ambience. Alvin Boyarsky and the Architectural Association
curators: Nadejda Bartels, Jan Howard, Igor Marjanović

2016 **Anime Architecture**
curator: Stefan Riekeles

Architectural Master Drawings from the Albertina
from the collection of the Albertina, Vienna, Austria;
curator: Dr Christian Benedik

Peter Cook. Retrospective
curators: Nadejda Bartels, Kristin Feireiss

2015 **Alexander Brodsky – Works**
curator: Daria Paramonova

American Perspectives: From Classic to Contemporary
curator: Sergei Tchoban

In Pursuit of Antiquity: Drawings by the Giants of British Neo-Classicism
from the collection of the Sir John Soane's Museum, London, UK;
curator: Jeremy Musson

2014 **Lebbeus Woods. On-Line**
curator: Christoph a. Kumpusch

L'hôtel particulier à Paris
(L'hôtel particulier in Paris)
from the collection of the École nationale supérieure des beaux-arts, Paris, France;
curator: Emmanuelle Brugerolles

New Acquisitions. Works on Paper. 1967–2013
curator: Nadejda Bartels

2013 **Architecture in Cultural Strife.
Russian and Soviet Architecture in Drawings. 1900–1953**
curator: Irina Sedova

Piranesi's Paestum – Master Drawings Uncovered
from the collection of the Sir John Soane's Museum, London, UK;
curator: Dr Jerzy J. Kierkúc-Bieliński

External Exhibitions
Tchoban Foundation
Museum for Architectural Drawing

2017 **Architecture de l'avant-garde Russe. Dessins de la Collection Sergei Tchoban**
(Architecture of the Russian avant-garde. Drawings from the Sergei Tchoban Collection)
curator: Prof Dr Jean-Louis Cohen;
Cabinet des dessins Jean Bonna, École nationale supérieure des beaux-arts,
Paris, France

2016 **Solo Italia. Architettura e paesaggio culturale. Disegni dal Settecento ad Oggi**
(Only Italy! Architecture and cultural landscape. Drawings of the 18th–21st centuries)
curators: Rita Bernini, Nina Markova, Galina Tzedrik;
exhibition by the Tchoban Foundation. Museum for Architectural Drawing,
the Istituto Centrale per la Grafica di Roma, and the Tretyakov Gallery;
Museo dell'Istituto Centrale per la Grafica, Rome, Italy

2015 **Treasure, Legacy: A Museum for Architectural Drawing**
curator: Prof Mark Morris;
Cornell University College of Architecture, Art and Planning, Ithaca, New York, USA

2014 **All about Italy! / Only Italy! Architectural Graphics of the 18th–21st centuries**
curators: Nina Markova, Irina Sedova;
Tretyakov Gallery, Moscow, Russia

2013 **Northern Vision. Master Drawings from the Tchoban Foundation**
curators: Nadejda Bartels, Dr Jerzy J. Kierkúc- Bieliński;
Sir John Soane's Museum, London, UK

2012   **Library of Architecture**
curator: Dmitry Ozerkov;
The Hermitage, Saint Petersburg, Russia

2011   **À la Source de l'antique. La Collection de Sergei Tchoban**
(To the source of antiquity. The Sergei Tchoban Collection)
curator: Emmanuelle Brugerolles;
Cabinet des dessins Jean Bonna, École nationale supérieure des beaux-arts, Paris, France

2010   **Architekturwelten. Sergei Tchoban – Zeichner und Sammler**
(Architectural worlds. Sergei Tchoban – draughtsman and collector)
curator: Eva-Maria Barkhofen;
Deutsches Architekturmuseum (DAM), Frankfurt am Main, Germany

The Golden Age of Architectural Graphic Art. Drawings by European Masters of the 18th–19th Centuries from the Sergei Tchoban Collection
curators: Vladimir Sedov, Irina Sedova;
Pushkin Museum of Fine Arts, Moscow, Russia

Awards

2020   **DAM Prize for Architecture 2020**
(Deutsches Architekturmuseum (DAM));
nomination;
project: Boxhagener Strasse, Berlin, Germany

Premio Internazionale Giacomo Quarenghi 2020
(Osservatorio Quarenghi);
Tchoban Foundation, Berlin, Germany

2019   **Global Architecture & Design Awards 2019**
(Rethinking the Future);
1st prize; category: Sports & Recreation (built);
project: Stadtbad Nauen, Nauen, Germany

Global Architecture & Design Awards 2019
(Rethinking the Future);
3rd prize; category: Commercial (built);
project: Boxhagener Strasse, Berlin, Germany

International Property Awards 2019
(International Property Media Ltd.);
World's Best Property 2019; category: World's Best;
project: Federation Complex, Moscow, Russia

International Property Awards Development 2019
(International Property Media Ltd.);
category: Best International Residential High-Rise Development;
project: Federation Complex, Moscow, Russia

The International Architecture Award 2019
(The Chicago Athenaeum: Museum of Architecture and Design, The European Centre for Architecture Art Design and Urban Studies);
project: Federation Tower, Moscow, Russia

2018 **Best Informal Drawing Award 2018 at Architecture in Perspective 33**
(The American Society of Architectural Illustrators (ASAI));
project: Way to the Top (office building in Moscow)

DAM Prize for Architecture 2018
(Deutsches Architekturmuseum (DAM));
nomination;
project: The White, Berlin, Germany

FIABCI Prix d'Excellence 2018
(The International Real Estate Federation);
Silver;
project: WineHouse, Moscow, Russia

First Athens Architecture Club 2018
(exhibition and competition held by the The Chicago Athenaeum: Museum of Architecture Design and The European Centre for Architecture Art Design and Urban Studies);
Gold Medal

MIPIM Awards 2018
(Marché International des Professionnels de l'immobilier);
finalist; category: Best Arena of the Year 2018;
project: Luzhniki Stadium, Moscow, Russia

Observational Best in Show Award 2018 at Architecture in Perspective 33
(The American Society of Architectural Illustrators (ASAI));
project: Old Delhi, 2018

2017 **Architecture Drawing Prize 2017**
(inaugural prize, WAF 2017);
honourable mention;
project: Dead-End 1

DAM Prize for Architecture 2017
(German Architecture Museum (DAM));
nomination;
project: Living Levels, Berlin, Germany

International Property Awards 2017–2018
(International Property Media Ltd.);
category: Best International Residential High-Rise Development;
project: Neva Towers, Moscow, Russia

Moscow City Prize for Architecture 2017
(City of Moscow);
diploma; category: Best Architectural and Urban-Planning Solution for an Office and Administration;
project: Building at Leningradsky Prospekt 31, Moscow, Russia

SportEngineering AWARD 2017
(SportEngineering);
project: Luzhniki Stadium, Moscow, Russia

Wienerberger Brick Award 2017
(Wienerberger GmbH);
nomination;
project: Klosterkirche Sankt Georg, Götschendorf, Germany

2016 **ARCHIWOOD Award 2016**
(Honka);
project: Russian Pavilion, EXPO 2015, Milan, Italy

IHM Prize 2016, GEPLANT + AUSGEFÜHRT
(GHM Gesellschaft für Handwerksmessen);
nomination;
project: Villa near Potsdam, Potsdam, Germany

IHP – Internationaler Hochhaus Preis 2016
(German Architecture Museum (DAM));
nomination;
project: Federation Complex, Moscow, Russia

PROESTATE Awards 2016
(PROESTATE International Real Estate Investment Forum);
Best Architectural Design of the Decade;
project: Nevsky City Hall (Government Quarter), Saint Petersburg, Russia

The International Architecture Award 2016
(The Chicago Athenaeum: Museum of Architecture Design and The European Centre for Architecture Art Design and Urban Studies);
project: Museum for Rural Labour, Zvizzhi, Russia

2015 Architecture in Perspective 30
(American Society of Architectural Illustrators (ASAI));
Informal Category Award;
project: Design for a film project

German Design Award 2015
(German Design Council);
winner; category: Excellent Communication Design – Architecture and Urban Space;
project: Museum for Architectural Drawing, Berlin, Germany

German Lighting Design Award 2015
(Hüthig GmbH);
project: Museum for Architectural Drawing, Berlin, Germany

Heinze ArchitektenAward 2015
(Heinze GmbH);
winner; category: Allure Non-Residential Construction;
project: Museum for Architectural Drawing, Berlin, Germany

IHM Preis 2015 GEPLANT + AUSGEFÜHRT
(GHM Gesellschaft für Handwerksmessen);
3rd prize;
project: Museum for Architectural Drawing, Berlin, Germany

MiesArch 2015
(Fundació Mies van der Rohe);
nomination;
project: Museum for Architectural Drawing, Berlin, Germany

The International Architecture Award 2015
(The Chicago Athenaeum: Museum of Architecture and Design and The European Centre for Architecture Art Design and Urban Studies);
project: INNSIDE by Meliá Hotel, Wolfsburg, Germany

2014 AIT Award – Best in Interior and Architecture 2014
(AIT-Dialog);
honourable mention; category: Public Building / Education;
project: Museum for Architectural Drawing, Berlin, Germany

Architizer A+Awards 2014
(Architizer LCC);
honourable mention; category: Museums;
project: Museum for Architectural Drawing, Berlin, Germany

DAM Architecture Award 2014
(Deutsches Architekturmuseum (DAM));
nomination; category: Best Buildings in and from Germany;
project: Museum for Architectural Drawing, Berlin, Germany

Jed Morse Juror Rendering Award 2014 at Architecture in Perspective 29
(American Society of Architectural Illustrators (ASAI));
project: Two Worlds No.1

Ken Roberts Memorial Delineation Competition
(KRob) 2014 (AIA Dallas);
jury citation; category: Professional Travel Sketch;
project: Santa Maria della Salute, Venice, 2012

The International Architecture Award 2014
(The Chicago Athenaeum: Museum of Architecture and Design and
The European Centre for Architecture Art Design and Urban Studies);
project: Museum for Architectural Drawing, Berlin, Germany

2013 **AR+D Emerging Architecture Awards 2013**
(The Architectural Review);
joint winner;
project: Museum for Architectural Drawing, Berlin, Germany

Bau des Jahres 2013
(german-architects.com);
2nd place;
project: Museum for Architectural Drawing, Berlin, Germany

Best of Year Awards 2013
(*Interior Design* magazine);
winner; category: Exhibition;
project: *i-city / i-land*, exhibition for the 13th Biennale of Architecture, Venice, Italy

Future projects Awards 2013
(*The Architectural Review*);
highly commended; category: Old & New;
project: Museum for Architectural Drawing, Berlin, Germany

Iconic Awards 2013
(German Design Council);
winner; Best of Best; category: Architecture – Public;
project: Museum for Architectural Drawing, Berlin, Germany

Iconic Awards 2013
(German Design Council)
winner; Best of Best; category: Architecture – Event/Exhibition;
project: *i-city / i-land*, exhibition for the 13th Biennale of Architecture, Venice, Italy

WAF Award 2013
(EMAP Publishing Limited);
highly commended; category: Culture;
project: Museum for Architectural Drawing, Berlin, Germany

2012 **3rd Biennale of Architecture, Moscow, 2012**
category: Architect of the Year;
Sergei Tchoban, together with Sergey Kuznetsov, SPEECH Tchoban & Kuznetsov

13th Biennale of Architecture, Venice, 2012
Special Mention;
project: Russian Pavilion (*i-city / i-land* exhibition), Venice, Italy

Best Office Award 2012
(officenext.ru);
Grand Prix;
project: interior design for the offices of VTB Group in the West Tower of the Federation Tower complex, Moscow, Russia

International Property Awards 2012
(International Property Media Ltd.);
winner; category: Best Office Architecture;
project: office building on Leninsky Prospekt, Moscow, Russia

2011

Award of the Russian Union of Architects 2011
(Russian Union of Architects);
Vasily Bazhenov Medal 2011

Building of the Year 2011
(*Made in Future* magazine);
project: office building on Leninsky Prospekt, Moscow, Russia

Glass in Architecture Award 2011
(Russian Union of Architects);
Gold Prize; category: New Build;
project: Saint Petersburg Plaza (business complex), Saint Petersburg, Russia

immobilienawardberlin 2011
(Berliner Volksbank, Eurohypo, Drees & Sommer, Jones Lang LaSalle, PWC, stöbe mehnert);
project: Hotel nhow Berlin, Berlin, Germany

The International Architecture Award 2011
(The Chicago Athenaeum: Museum of Architecture and Design and The European Centre for Architecture Art Design and Urban Studies);
project: Hamburger Hof, Berlin, Germany

2010

The International Architecture Award 2010
(The Chicago Athenaeum: Museum of Architecture and Design and The European Centre for Architecture Art Design and Urban Studies);
project: Chabad Lubavitch synagogue and community centre, Berlin, Germany

2009

Building of the Year 2009
(*Made in Future* magazine);
project: Benois Business Centre, Saint Petersburg, Russia

FIABCI Prix d'Excellence 2009
(International Real Estate Federation);
winner; category: Offices;
project: Federation Complex, Moscow, Russia

International Architecture Award ArchiP 2009
(ArchiP);
winner; category: Public Building – Tradition;
project: Chabad Lubavitch synagogue and community centre, Berlin, Germany

2008 Award of the Russian Union of Architects 2008
Gold Diploma; category: Buildings;
project: House by the Sea (residential complex), Saint Petersburg, Russia

2005 German Natural Stone Award 2005
(DNV e.V., Association of German Architects (BDA));
honourable mention;
project: DomAquarée, Berlin, Germany

2004 Award of the Saint Petersburg Union of Architects 2004
(Architekton);
Grand Prix;
project: design for House by the Sea (residential complex), Saint Petersburg, Russia

2003 ARCH Moscow 2003
(Expo Park);
Critics' Award; category: Exhibition;
project: design for Idee, Prozess, Raum (Idea, process, space), Berlin, Germany

2002 German Interior-Architecture Award 2002
(Association of German Interior Architects (BDIA));
special mention;
project: Kino Cubix, Berlin, Germany

2000 ARCH Moscow 2000
(Expo Park);
Critics' Award; category: Exhibition;
project: curation, design, and organisation of Raum für Kunst (Room for art)

1999 BDA Hamburg Architecture Prize 1999
(BDA Hamburg);
2nd prize;
project: Trabrennbahn residential complex, Hamburg-Farmsen, Max-Herz-Ring, Hamburg, Germany

1998 German Urban Planning Prize 1998
(formerly the Walter Hesselbach Prize; BFG Bank AG);
special mention;
project: Trabrennbahn residential complex, Hamburg-Farmsen, Max-Herz-Ring, Hamburg, Germany

Publications

2019 Förster, Yorck; Gräwe, Christina; Schmal, Peter Cachola (eds.)
Architekturführer Deutschland 2020
(Architecture guide Germany 2020)
DOM Publishers, Berlin, 2019, pp. 56–57

Haubrich, Rainer
Das Scheunenviertel
Insel, Berlin, 2019, pp. 144–147

Feddersen, Eckhard (ed.)
Skizzen Havelberg
(Sketches Havelberg)
Self-published, Berlin, 2019

Tchoban, Sergei; Voss, Ekkehard
Tchoban Voss Architekten / Tchoban Voss Architects
JOVIS, Berlin, 2019

2018 Elkina, Maria
Архитектура. Как ее понимать
(Architecture. How to understand it.)
Drawings: Sergei Tchoban
Арка / Arka, Saint Petersburg, 2018

Martovitskaya, Anna
Architekturführer Berlin
(Architecture guide Berlin)
DOM Publishers, Berlin, 2018, pp. 34, 36, 110, 116, 118

Tchoban, Sergei; Martovitskaya, Anna
Три дня в Амстердаме. Краткий путеводитель в рисунках
(Three days in Amsterdam. Brief guide in the form of drawings)
Ripol Classic, Moscow, 2018

Tchoban, Sergei; Martovitskaya, Anna
Три дня в Париже. Краткий путеводитель в рисунках
(Three days in Paris. Brief guide in the form of drawings)
Ripol Classic, Moscow, 2018

Tchoban, Sergei; Martovitskaya, Anna
Три дня в Праге. Краткий путеводитель в рисунках
(Three days in Prague. Brief guide in the form of drawings)
Ripol Classic, Moscow, 2018

Tchoban, Sergei; Martovitskaya, Anna
Три дня в Москва. Краткий путеводитель в рисунках
(Three days in Moscow. Brief guide in the form of drawings)
Ripol Classic, Moscow, 2019

2017 Tchoban, Sergei; Sedov, Vladimir
**30:70. Architecture as a Balancing Act /
30:70. Architektur als Balanceakt / 30:70. 建筑平衡行为论**
DOM Publishers, Berlin, 2017

Tchoban, Sergei; Sedov, Vladimir
30:70. архитектура как баланс сил
(30:70. Architecture as a balancing act)
Novoe literaturnoe obozrenie, Moscow, 2017

Förster, Yorck; Gräwe, Christina; Schmal, Peter Cachola (eds.)
Architekturführer Deutschland 2017
(Architecture guide Germany 2017)
DOM Publishers, Berlin, 2017, pp. 85, 113

Tatlin Mono (ed.)
TATLIN Plan #29 Деловой квартал «Невская ратуша»
(TATLIN Plan #29 Nevsky City Hall Business District)
Izdatelstvo Tatlin, Moscow, 2017

Tchoban, Sergei; Martovitskaya, Anna
Три дня во Флоренции. Краткий путеводитель в рисунках
(Three days in Florence. Brief guide in the form of drawings)
Ripol Classic, Moscow, 2017

Tchoban, Sergei; Martovitskaya, Anna
Три дня в Риме. Краткий путеводитель в рисунках
(Three days in Rome. Brief guide in the form of drawings)
Ripol Classic, Moscow, 2017

Tchoban, Sergei; Martovitskaya, Anna
Три дня в Венеции. Краткий путеводитель в рисунках
(Three days in Venice. Brief guide in the form of drawings)
Ripol Classic, Moscow, 2017

2016 Schendel, Dominik; Meuser, Philipp (eds.)
Architekturführer Berlin. Zwölf Touren durch die deutsche Hauptstadt
(Architecture guide Berlin. Twelve tours through the German capital)
DOM Publishers, Berlin, 2016, pp. 145, 157, 230, 354

Tatlin Mono (ed.)
TATLIN Plan #17 Музей архитектурного рисунка
(TATLIN Plan #17 Museum for Architectural Drawing)
Izdatelstvo Tatlin, Moscow, 2016

2015 Johenning, Heike Maria
Architekturführer Sankt Petersburg
(Architecture guide / Saint Petersburg)
DOM Publishers, Berlin, 2014, pp. 17, 314, 325, 335f., 347f., 350f.

Braun, Markus Sebastian; van Uffelen, Chris (eds.)
Atlas of European Architecture
Braun Publishing, Berlin, 2015, pp. 494–497

Tchoban, Sergei
Die Kunst der Architekturzeichnung
(The art of architectural drawing)
in: Meuser, Natascha,
Construction and Design Manual / Drawing for Architects
DOM Publishers, Berlin, 2015, pp. 38–49, 120–125

Molinari, Luca (ed.)
Sergei Tchoban, Architecture Drawings
Skira, Milan, 2015

2014 Kramer, Sibylle (ed.)
Exhibition Designs
Braun Publishing, Berlin, 2014, pp. 30, 178

Jaeger, Falk (ed.)
nps tchoban voss, Baukultur wahren – Gestaltung wagen
Cultural Continuity – Design Progression
JOVIS, Berlin, 2014

2013 van Uffelen, Chris (ed.)
Apartment Buildings
Braun Publishing, Berlin, 2013, pp. 294, 388

Tatlin Mono (ed.)
SPEECH Tchoban & Kuznetsov
Izdatelstvo Tatlin, Moscow, 2013

2012 Jaeger, Falk (ed.)
Architekturtransfers / Architectural Transfers, SPEECH. Tchoban & Kuznetsov
JOVIS, Berlin, 2012

van Uffelen, Chris (ed.)
Façades
Braun Publishing, Berlin, 2012, pp. 114, 188

van Uffelen, Chris (ed.)
Skyscrapers
Braun Publishing, Berlin, 2012, pp. 54, 80, 278

Stimmann, Hans (ed.); Schäche, Wolfgang; Ouwerkerk, Erik-Jan
Zukunft des Kulturforums. Ein Abgesang auf die Insel der Objekte
(The Future of the Kulturforum. A swansong to the island of objects)
DOM Publishers, Berlin, 2012, pp. 178–185

2011 Meuser, Philipp; Knoch Peter
Architekturführer Moskau
(Architecture guide Moscow)
DOM Publishers, Berlin, 2011, p. 382

Haubrich, Rainer; Hoffmann, Hans Wolfgang; Meuser, Philipp;
van Uffelen, Chris; Braun, Markus Sebastian (eds.)
Berlin – der Architekturführer
(Berlin: the architecture guide)
Braun Publishing, Berlin, 2011 (first edition), 2015, p. 322

van Uffelen, Chris (ed.)
Re-Use Architecture
Braun Publishing, Berlin, 2011, pp. 172, 236, 290, 350

2010 Barkhofen, Eva-Maria (ed.)
Architectural Worlds. Sergei Tchoban – Draftsman and Collector
JOVIS, Berlin, 2010

Chipova, Irina (ed.)
Factory Russia. Фабрика Россия /
Vyshny Volochok Transformations. Вышний Волочек Трансформации
The Ministry of Culture of The Russian Federation, Moscow, 2010

Nance, Kevin (ed.)
Sergei Tchoban: Architecture / Art
The Images Publishing Group, Mulgrave, Victoria, 2010

2009 Dubrau, Dorothee (ed.),
publication on behalf of the administration of Berlin Mitte
Architekturführer Berlin-Mitte
(Architecture guide Berlin Mitte), 2 volumes
DOM Publishers, Berlin, 2009, pp. 128, 169, 374, 441, 532

van Uffelen, Chris (ed.)
Cinema Architecture
Braun Publishing, Berlin, 2009, pp. 12–15

van Uffelen, Chris (ed.)
Malls and Department Stores
Braun Publishing, Berlin, 2009, pp. 92, 282

Tatlin Mono
Sergej Tchoban, 1997–2009
Izdatelstvo Tatlin, Moscow, 2009

2008 Jaeger, Falk (ed.)
nps tchoban voss: Vom Detail zum Stadtraum / From Detail to Urban Space
Birkhäuser, Basel, 2008

2007 Lee, Vinny
Schwimmbecken und Whirlpools für drinnen und draußen
(Swimming pools and whirlpools for indoors and outdoors)
DVA, Munich, 2007, pp. 28-29

van Uffelen, Chris (ed.)
Offices
Braun Publishing, Berlin, 2007, pp. 54, 192, 202, 344

2006 Walter, Jörn (ed.)
Pläne Projekte Bauten Hamburg: Architektur und Städtebau 2005 bis 2015
(Plans projects buildings Hamburg: architecture and urban planning 2005-2015)
Braun Publishing, Berlin, 2006, pp. 42, 208, 250, 258

Dörries, Cornelia; Platea, Andrea
Raumkunst
(Space art)
Braun Publishing, Berlin, 2004, (first edition), 2006, pp. 56-59

2005 Jaeger, Falk (ed.)
Der Kopf des Architekten: Zeichnungen und Baukunst von Sergei Tchoban
(The architect's head: drawings and architecture by Sergei Tchoban)
JOVIS, Berlin, 2005

Trauenstein, Magnus
Hotels in Germany
Braun Publishing, Berlin, 2005, pp. 90-95

2004 Architektenkammer Berlin (ed.)
Architektur Berlin 04. Über die Vereinbarkeit von Bauen und Architektur
(Architecture Berlin 04. On the compatibility of building and architecture)
Braun Publishing, Berlin, 2004, pp. 34, 94

Meuser, Philipp (ed.)
Berlin im Fluss / Floating Berlin
Braun Publishing, Berlin, 2004, p. 54

Zohlen, Gerwin
DOMAQUARÈE. Sergei Tchoban, nps tchoban voss architekten
(DOMAQUARÈE. Sergei Tchoban, nps tchoban voss architekten)
Junius, Hamburg, 2004

Andrews, Jonathan
Handgezeichnete Visionen. Eine Sammlung aus deutschen Architekturbüros
(Hand-drawn visions. A collection of German architecture firms)
Braun Publishing, Berlin, 2004, pp. 236-247

ifa-Galerie Berlin
**STADTanSICHTEN – Planschrank Moskau /
ВИД(ение) ГОРОДА – Чертежный архив Москвы**
(CITYvision/VIEWS – Moscow Drawing Archive)
Braun Publishing, Berlin, 2004

2003   Yee, Rendow
Architectural Drawing. A Visual Compendium of Types and Methods. Second Edition
Wiley, Hoboken, New Jersey, 2003, pp. 374–375

Feireiss, Kristin (ed.)
Handgezeichnete Welten / Hand-Drawn Worlds
JOVIS, Berlin, 2003, pp. 160–167

2000   Burden, Ernest
Visionary Architecture. Unbuilt Works of the Imagination
McGraw-Hill Professional, New York, 2000, pp. 196–197

1999   Grice, Gordon
The Art of Architectural Illustration 3
Rockport Publishers, Rockport, Massachusetts, 1999, pp. 212–217

1997   Chen, John S. M.
Architecture in Color Drawings
McGraw-Hill Companies, New York, 1997, p. 100

Schaller, Thomas Wells
The Art of Architectural Drawing. Imagination & Technique
Wiley, Hoboken, New Jersey, 1997, p. 152

Barr, Vilma; Antman, Dani
The Illustrated Room. 20th-Century Interior Design Rendering
McGraw-Hill Professional, New York, 1997, p. 239

1996   Grice, Gordon
The Art of Architectural Illustration 2
Rockport Publishers, Rockport, Massachusetts, 1996, pp. 218–223

1993   Perlmann, Robert W.
The Art of Architectural Illustration
Rockport Publishers, Rockport, Massachusetts, 1993, pp. 200–203

Projects and Partners

Page 14 Federation Complex, Moscow, 2017; Prof. Peter P. Schweger, Sergei Tchoban; Matthias Dahlmann, Valeria Kashirina, Matthias Lassen, Paul Olufs, Lidia Rtiseva, Team TCHOBAN VOSS Architekten: Stefan Barme, Jörn Frenzel, Peter Galonska, Philipp Gubkin, Christoph Heimermann, Natalia von Krüchten, Anissa Landgraf, Ines Lehmann, Anna Linda-Kinder, Igor Markov, Katja Redmann, Anna Sacharowa, Stefanie Seegerer, Steffen Thauer, Pavel Zemskov; Sergey Kuznetsov; Team SPEECH: Kirill Chaljavsky, Vladimir Chaljavsky, Alexandra Glotova, Sergey Glubokin, Andrej Perlich, Lubov Shirokova, Tatyana Zhokhova

Page 18 Russian Monastery of St George, Götschendorf, 2017; Sergei Tchoban; Philipp Bauer, Karsten Waldschmidt, Team TCHOBAN VOSS Architekten: Simon Bange, Katja Fuks, Dirk Kollendt

Page 21 Russian Pavilion, Milan Expo 2015, Milan, 2015; Sergei Tchoban, Alexej Ilin; Team SPEECH: Marina Kuznetskaja, Andrej Perlich

Page 30 The Bright Way. 19.17, MAT (Moscow Art Theatre), Moscow, 2017; director: Aleksandr Molochnikov, stage design: Sergei Tchoban, Agniya Sterligova

Page 33 The Bright Way. 19.17, MAT (Moscow Art Theatre), Moscow, 2017; director: Aleksandr Molochnikov, stage design: Sergei Tchoban, Agniya Sterligova

Pages 36-37 Hamburger Hof, Berlin, 2010; Sergei Tchoban; Frederik-Sebastian Scholz, Team TCHOBAN VOSS Architekten: Christian Barwe, Anja Koch

Pages 38-39 Living Levels, Berlin, 2015; Sergei Tchoban; Philipp Bauer, Karsten Waldschmidt, Team TCHOBAN VOSS Architekten: Christoph Heimermann, Stephan Luda-Scharping, Kenan Ozan, Anja Schroth

Pages 40-41 Music- and Lifestyle Hotel nhow, Berlin, 2010; Sergei Tchoban; Axel Binder, Team TCHOBAN VOSS Architekten: Natalia von Krüchten, Andrea Moritz, Kenan Ozan, Manuela Peth

Pages 42-43 Chabad Lubavitch synagogue and community centre, Berlin, 2007; Sergei Tchoban; Frederik-Sebastian Scholz, Team TCHOBAN VOSS Architekten: Anja Koch, Anja Schroth

Pages 46-47 Chabad Lubavitch synagogue and community centre, Berlin, 2007; Sergei Tchoban; Frederik-Sebastian Scholz, Team TCHOBAN VOSS Architekten: Anja Koch, Anja Schroth

Pages 50-52 Office TCHOBAN VOSS Architekten, Berlin, 2002; Sergei Tchoban; Stephan Lohre, Team TCHOBAN VOSS Architekten: Daniel Brand, Norbert Krenz.

Page 56 City Quartier DomAquarée, Berlin, 2004; Sergei Tchoban; Axel Binder, Ulrike Graefenhain, Stephan Lohre, Manfred Treiling, Team TCHOBAN VOSS Architekten: Anna von Abendroth, Philipp Bauer, Charlie Becker, Alexandra Behrens, Konrad Benstz, Roland Frank, Christian Graulich, Bernward Grützner, Antje Kalus, Anja Koch, Ralf Krausfeld, Adrian Lachowicz, Matthias Lassen, Jan-Henning Neske, Julia Neumann, Laurent Ngoc, Fabiana Pedretti, Anja Schroth, Steffen Schulz, Peter Sinnemann, Juliane Sprodel, Katharina Stranz, Christian Strauss, Angela Tohtz

Page 58 Office Building at Leninsky Prospect, Moscow, 2010; Sergei Tchoban, Sergey Kuznetsov; Team SPEECH: Sergey Glubokin, Anastasia Kozireva, Tatjana Lokteva, Evgenia Murinetz, Andrej Perlich, Tatjana Varuchina

Page 60 Granatny Alley Residences, Moscow, 2010; Sergei Tchoban, Sergey Kuznetsov; Team TCHOBAN VOSS Architekten: Valeria Kashirina, Paul Olufs, Pavel Zemskov; Team SPEECH: Sergey Arytunov, Anatolij Borisov, Vladimir Chaljavsky, Angelika Gorobetz, Vyacheslav Kazul, Julia Kotlyar, Anastasia Kozireva, Anna Kuznetsova, Olga Michalchenko, Andrew Perlich, Kristina Skudnova, Anastasia Sokolnikova, Teodor Stoljarov

Page 61 Kronprinzengärten, Berlin, 2017; Sergei Tchoban; Stephan Lohre, Karsten Waldschmidt, Team TCHOBAN VOSS Architekten: Birgit Köder, Dirk Kollendt, Andrea Moritz, Fabiana Pedretti, Manuela Peth, Katja Redmann, Wolfgang Tancke, Sören Vohs

Page 62 Seasons Ensemble, Saint Petersburg, 2013; Sergei Tchoban; Team TCHOBAN VOSS Architekten: Silvia Grischkat, Valeria Kashirina, Paul Olufs, Eugen Pfeil, Frederik-Sebastian Scholz, Pavel Zemskov

Pages 69-70 Pavilion for the Tretyakov Gallery to demonstrate "ProYavlenie", a media project which reproduces all the stages of the creation of The Appearance Before the People, the famous painting by Aleksandr Ivanov, Moscow, 2017; Sergei Tchoban, Agniya Sterligova

Page 76 Nevskaya Ratusha (Nevsky City Hall), Saint Petersburg, 2016; Yevgeny Gerasimov, Sergei Tchoban; Tatjana Komaldinova, Zoja Petrova, Team Gerasimov and Partners: Irina Bakhorina, Natalia Bezborodova, Alexander Gvozdik, Tatjana Kuznetsova, Oleg Manov, Maria Orlova-Scheyner, Ekaterina Reznikova, Olga Tunova; Valeria Kashirina, Frederik-Sebastian Scholz, Pavel Zemskov, Team TCHOBAN VOSS Architekten: René Hoch, Ingo Schwarzweller, Ramona Schwarzweller; Andrej Perlich, Team SPEECH: Sergey Arutyunov, Olga Berlyand, Aliya Boranbaeva, Maksim Grishanov, Andrey Kabanov, Vyacheslav Kazul, Anna Khmelenina, Anastasiya Kozyreva, Mariya Kutovski, Marina Kuznetsova, Yuliya Lavrova, Artem Lisitsyn, Tatyana Lokteva, Tatyana Lyubimova, Olga Nikitina,

Larisa Panasenko, Anastasiya Plotnikova, Yelena Pluzhnik, Mariya Rasskazova, Yekaterina Sennikova, Yana Shestikhina, Svetlana Shilova, Kristina Skudnova, Anastasiya Tychinina, Tatyana Zhukova

Pages 78-79 Water Sports Palace, Kazan, 2012; Sergei Tchoban, Sergey Kuznetsov; Nikolay Gordushin, Team SPEECH: Georgy Glebov, Tatiana Logunova, Alexey Shubkin, Tatjana Varuchina

Page 85 The apartment of Sergei Tchoban, Saint Petersburg, 2017; Sergei Tchoban, Anna Reznik

Page 106 Kronprinzengärten, Berlin, 2017; Sergei Tchoban, Stephan Lohre, Karsten Waldschmidt, Team TCHOBAN VOSS Architekten: Birgit Köder, Dirk Kollendt, Andrea Moritz, Fabiana Pedretti, Manuela Peth, Katja Redmann, Wolfgang Tancke, Sören Vohs

Pages 120-121 Ackerstrasse 29, Berlin, 2016; Sergei Tchoban; Philipp Bauer, Team TCHOBAN VOSS Architekten: Katja Fuks, Natalia von Krüchten, Anissa Landgraf, Kenan Ozan, Karsten Waldschmidt

Pages 122-123 The White, Berlin, 2016; Sergei Tchoban; Philipp Bauer, Team TCHOBAN VOSS Architekten: Anissa Landgraf, Magdalena Schwalke, Karsten Waldschmidt

Pages 124-125 Boxhagener Strasse, Berlin, 2018; Sergei Tchoban; Stephan Lohre, Team TCHOBAN VOSS Architekten: Virginie Mommens, Katja Redmann, Anja Schroth, Katharina Stranz

Page 126 Business House Langenzipen, Saint Petersburg, 2006; Sergei Tchoban; Valeria Kashirina, Frederik-Sebastian Scholz, Team TCHOBAN VOSS Architekten: Silvia Grischkat, Philipp Gubkin, Eugen Pfeil

Page 127 Cubix CineStar Alexanderplatz, Berlin, 2001; Sergei Tchoban; Philipp Bauer, Stephan Lohre, Team TCHOBAN VOSS Architekten, Ulrike Graefenhain, Julia Neumann

Pages 130-131 Wine House residential complex, Moscow, 2017; Sergei Tchoban, Igor Chlenov; Team SPEECH: Alexander Christov, Anna Deryabina, Marina Digileva, Denis Golikov, Sergey Popov, Alexandra Rusakova, Oleg Zolotykh; Team TPO Reserve: Ivan Anokhin, Denis Chernov, Dmitry Kazakov, Darya Khomiakova, Anna Larionova, Anna Romanova, Marina Shershova, Anna Vartapetova

Page 136 Luzhniki Stadium, Moscow, 2017; Sergei Tchoban, Nikolay Gordushin, Alexey Shubkin; Team SPEECH: Ekaterina Chernykh, Alexander Fedorov, Liliya Korneeva, Olga Lipis, Anastasiya Loginova, Svetlana Lozhkina, Elena Medvedeva, Elizaveta Serova

Page 143 Business House Langenzipen, Saint Petersburg, 2006; Sergei Tchoban; Valeria Kashirina, Frederik-Sebastian Scholz, Team TCHOBAN VOSS Architekten: Silvia Grischkat, Philipp Gubkin, Eugen Pfeil

Page 154 Open Borders. Bienal Internacional de Arte Contemporânea de Curitiba 2019, Oscar Niemeyer Museum, Curitiba, 2019; curator: Tereza de Arruda, co-curator: Esenija Bannan

Page 155 Sergei Tchoban: Contrasting Harmony of the City, Museum of Architecture, Wrocław, 2018; curators: Esenija Bannan, Jolanta Gromadzka

Page 157 Dreams of Frozen Music - The Architectural Drawings of Sergei Tchoban, Tokyo Art Museum, Tokyo, 2018; curator: Jan-Philipp Frühsorge

Pages 172-173 Aedes Extension Pavilion (former Galerie Arndt), Berlin, 1999; Sergei Tchoban, Philipp Bauer, Stephan Lohre (TCHOBAN VOSS Architekten); curators: Sergei Tchoban, Valeria Kashirina

Pages 176-177 Architectural Worlds. Sergei Tchoban: Draftsman and Collector, Deutsches Architekturmuseum (DAM), Frankfurt am Main, Germany, 2010; curator: Eva-Maria Barkhofen, exhibition design: Valeria Kashirina

Pages 179-181 i-city / i-land, Russian Pavilion, 13th Venice Biennale of Architecture, Venice, 2012; commissar: Grigory Revzin, curator: Sergei Tchoban, co-curators: Valeria Kashirina, Sergey Kuznetsov

Page 183 Roma Aeterna. Masterworks of the Vatican Pinacoteca, Tretyakov Gallery, Moscow, 2016; exhibition design: Sergei Tchoban, Agniya Sterligova

Pages 184-185 Giorgio de Chirico. Metaphysical Insights, Tretyakov Gallery, Moscow, 2017; exhibition design: Sergei Tchoban, Agniya Sterligova

Page 186 La Russia e fatta a modo suo (Russian pilgrimage), Vatican Pinacoteca, Vatican, 2018; exhibition design: Sergei Tchoban, Agniya Sterligova

Pages 188-189 Jan Vanriet – Losing face, Jewish Museum and Tolerance Centre, Moscow, 2015; exhibition design: Sergei Tchoban, Agniya Sterligova

Pages 190-191 Gary Tatintsian Gallery, Moscow, 2013; Sergei Tchoban, Andrej Perlich; Team SPEECH: Maxim Grishanov, Anastasiya Kozyreva, Mariya Rasskazova, Anastasiya Sokolnikova

Pages 192-193 The Forge of Great Architecture. Soviet Competitions of the 1920s–50s, Shchusev Museum of Architecture, Moscow, 2014; exhibition design: Sergei Tchoban, Agniya Sterligova

Pages 194-195 U-Cloud, exhibition by INTERNI, Milan, 2014; Sergei Tchoban, Sergey Kuznetsov, Agniya Sterligova

Pages 196-197 Living Line, exhibition by INTERNI, Milan, 2015; Sergei Tchoban, Sergey Kuznetsov, Agniya Sterligova

Pages 198-199 STADTanSICHTEN – Planschrank Moskau / ВИД(ение) ГОРОДА – Чертежный архив Москвы (CITYvision/VIEWS – Moscow Drawing Archive), ifa-Galerie, Berlin, 2004; curator and exhibition design: Sergei Tchoban, co-curators: Valeria Kashirina, Julia Neumann

Pages 200-201 Project SPEECH, Multimedia Art Museum, Moscow, 2016; exhibition design: Sergei Tchoban, Agniya Sterligova, curator: Anna Martovitskaya

Pages 210-211 Museum for Rural Labour, Zvizzhi, Kaluga, 2015; Sergei Tchoban, Agniya Sterligova

Pages 214-215 Museum for Rural Labour, Zvizzhi, Kaluga, 2015; Sergei Tchoban, Agniya Sterligova

Pages 226-229 Tchoban Foundation. Museum for Architectural Drawing, Berlin, 2013; Sergei Tchoban, Sergey Kuznetsov (SPEECH); Philipp Bauer, Team TCHOBAN VOSS Architekten: Nadja Fedorova, Katja Fuks, Ulrike Graefenhain, Dirk Kollendt

Pages 235-237 Tchoban Foundation. Museum for Architectural Drawing, Berlin, 2013; Sergei Tchoban, Sergey Kuznetsov (SPEECH); Philipp Bauer, Team TCHOBAN VOSS Architekten: Nadja Fedorova, Katja Fuks, Ulrike Graefenhain, Dirk Kollendt

Page 249-251 Tchoban Foundation. Museum for Architectural Drawing, Berlin, 2013; Sergei Tchoban, Sergey Kuznetsov (SPEECH); Philipp Bauer, Team TCHOBAN VOSS Architekten: Nadja Fedorova, Katja Fuks, Ulrike Graefenhain, Dirk Kollendt

Copyrights

P. 14	© SPEECH, Photo: Dmitry Chistoprudov
P. 18	© Lev Chestakov
P. 21	© Roland Halbe, rolandhalbe.eu
P. 26	© Lev Chestakov
P. 29	© Greg Bannan
P. 30	© Tchoban Foundation
P. 30	© SPEECH, Photo: Vasily Bulanov
P. 32	© Tchoban Foundation
P. 33	© SPEECH, Photo: Vasily Bulanov
PP. 36–41	© Roland Halbe, rolandhalbe.eu
P. 42	© Julia Jungfer
P. 44	© Julia Jungfer
P. 46	© Julia Jungfer
P. 47	© Christian Gahl
PP. 50–51	© Lev Chestakov
P. 52	© Claus Graubner
P. 56	© Anke Müllerklein
P. 58	© SPEECH, Photo: Yuri Palmin
P. 60	© SPEECH, Photo: Yuri Palmin
P. 61	© Roland Halbe, rolandhalbe.eu
P. 62	© SPEECH, Photo: Aleksey Naroditsky
P. 65	© Lev Chestakov
PP. 68–70	© SPEECH, Photo: Vasily Bulanov
PP. 72–73	© Archive TCHOBAN VOSS Architekten
P. 75	© Tchoban Foundation
P. 76	© SPEECH, Photo: Andrey Belimov-Guschin
PP. 78–79	© SPEECH, Photo: Ilya Ivanov
P. 82	© Lev Chestakov
P. 85	© Patricia Parinejad
P. 86	© Tchoban Foundation
PP. 88–91	© Tchoban Foundation
P. 93–94	© Tchoban Foundation
P. 98	© Tchoban Foundation
PP. 100–105	© Tchoban Foundation
P. 106	© Roland Halbe, rolandhalbe.eu
PP. 110–112	© Tchoban Foundation
P. 116	© DOM Publishers, Design: Masako Tomokiyo
PP. 120–123	© Werner Huthmacher
PP. 124–125	© Roland Halbe, rolandhalbe.eu
P. 126	© Bernhard Kroll
P. 127	© Florian Bolk
P. 128	© Tchoban Foundation
PP. 130–131	© SPEECH, Photo: Dmitry Chebanenko
P. 132	© Peter Cook Collection
P. 135	© Tchoban Foundation
P. 136	© SPEECH, Photo: Dmitry Chistoprudov
P. 143	© Bernhard Kroll
PP. 144–145	© Tchoban Foundation
P. 148	© Lev Chestakov
P. 153	© Sergei Tchoban Collection
PP. 154–155	© Greg Bannan
P. 157	© Greg Bannan
P. 159	© Lev Chestakov
PP. 162–163	© Tchoban Foundation
PP. 166–167	© Sergei Tchoban Collection
P. 169	© Sergei Tchoban Collection
PP. 172–173	© Claus Graubner
P. 174	© Tchoban Foundation
PP. 176–177	© DAM, Photo: Uwe Dettmar
P. 179	© SPEECH
PP. 180–181	© Patricia Parinejad
P. 183	© SPEECH, Photo: Ilya Ivanov
PP. 184–185	© SPEECH, Photo: Dmitry Chebanenko
PP. 186–187	© SPEECH, Photo: Vasily Bulanov
PP. 188–189	© SPEECH, Photo: Danila Remizov
PP. 190–193	© SPEECH, Photo: Aleksey Naroditsky
PP. 194–195	© SPEECH, Photo: Anna Minaeva
PP. 196–197	© SPEECH, Photo: Aleksey Naroditsky
PP. 198–199	© Ebba Dangschat, mittelstandimportrait.de
PP. 200–201	© SPEECH, Photo: Vasily Bulanov
P. 204	© Lev Chestakov
P. 206	© JOVIS Verlag, Design: Sophie Bleifuß
P. 209	© Tchoban Foundation
PP. 210–211	© SPEECH, Photo: Dmitry Chebanenko
P. 213	© Tchoban Foundation
PP. 214–215	© SPEECH, Photo: Dmitry Chebanenko
PP. 217–219	© Tchoban Foundation
P. 221	© Archive TCHOBAN VOSS Architekten
P. 223	© Tchoban Foundation
P. 226	© Archive TCHOBAN VOSS Architekten
PP. 227–229	© Roland Halbe, rolandhalbe.eu
P. 233	© Sergei Tchoban Collection
PP. 235–236	© Patricia Parinejad
P. 237	© Roland Halbe, rolandhalbe.eu
P. 238	© Isabel Robson
P. 241	© Michaela Schöpke
P. 244	© SPEECH, Photo: Elena Petuchova
P. 247	© Roland Halbe, rolandhalbe.eu
P. 249	© Roland Halbe, rolandhalbe.eu
PP. 250–251	© Patricia Parinejad
P. 255	© Luke Hayes
P. 257	© Erik-Jan Ouwerkerk
P. 259	© Lev Chestakov

Imprint

Editor
Kristin Feireiss

Translation
Gareth Davies

Copy editor
Sophie Lovell

Graphic design
Carmen Maria Traud

Pre-press, printing and binding
DZA Druckerei zu Altenburg GmbH, Thuringia

© 2021 Park Books AG, Zurich

© for the texts: the authors

© for the images: see copyrights page

Park Books

Niederdorfstrasse 54

8001 Zurich

Switzerland

www.park-books.com

Park Books is being supported by the Federal Office of Culture with a general subsidy for the years 2021–2024.

All rights reserved; no part of this publication may be reproduced, stored in a retrieval system or transmitted in any form or by any means, electronic, mechanical, photocopying, recording, or otherwise, without the prior written consent of the publisher.

ISBN 978-3-03860-205-7